"D"—as his friends call him—has provided a terrific exposition of a much-neglected book of the New Testament. This is an informative, readable, and practical exposition of 2 Peter that is ideal for pastors, preachers, and study groups.

MICHAEL F. BIRD
academic dean, lecturer in theology,
Ridley College,
Melbourne, Australia

The question "What kind of people should you be?" is one that should be asked by the people of God in every generation. In this accessible primer, Donald Morcom shows how the neglected book of 2 Peter asks this question of the early church and of us. At the same time understandable for lay Christians and helpful for Christian scholars, this is the rare book that will serve people in the church no matter what their vocation or level of prior knowledge about the Bible. I highly recommend it not only to those interested in 2 Peter but to anyone who hopes to follow Christ in this challenging age.

MATTHEW Y. EMERSON
professor of religion, dean,
Hobbs College of Theology and Ministry,
Oklahoma Baptist University

T0317089

In this timely and accessible volume, Donald Morcom helps the honest, inquiring student of God's word to grapple with the question of what it means to live as the people of God in this world. The combination of faithful exegesis of the text of 2 Peter along with valuable insights into both the apostle's world and the world of today sets the stage well for a contemporary application that encourages the readers to understand the foundations of their faith. The reflection questions at the end of each section further encourage readers to see how God's word should be shaping the thinking and behavior of all who have received this precious faith.

PETER FRANCIS
principal,
Malyon Theological College,
Brisbane, Australia

LIVING IN GOD'S TRUE STORY

2 PETER

Other titles in the Transformative Word series

Visit lexhampress.com/transformative-word

The Universal Story: Genesis 1–11
by Dru Johnson

Freed to Be God's Family: The Book of Exodus
by Mark R. Glanville

Deserting the King: The Book of Judges
by David J. H. Beldman

Finding God in the Margins: The Book of Ruth
by Carolyn Custis James

Glimpsing the Mystery: The Book of Daniel
by Barbara M. Leung Lai

God Behind the Scenes: The Book of Esther
by Wayne K. Barkhuizen

When You Want to Yell at God: The Book of Job
by Craig G. Bartholomew

Walking in God's Wisdom: The Book of Proverbs
by Benjamin T. Quinn

Faith Amid the Ruins: The Book of Habakkuk
by Heath A. Thomas

Revealing the Heart of Prayer: The Gospel of Luke
by Craig G. Bartholomew

Together for the World: The Book of Acts
by Michael R. Wagenman

Transformed in Christ: 1 Corinthians
by Ron Elsdon and William Olhausen

Cutting Ties with Darkness: 2 Corinthians
by John D. Barry

Living Doctrine: The Book of Titus
by Daniel L. Akin

Christ Above All: The Book of Hebrews
by Adrio König

Between the Cross and the Throne: The Book of Revelation
by Matthew Y. Emerson

LIVING IN GOD'S TRUE STORY

2 PETER

TRANSFORMATIVE WORD

DONALD L. MORCOM

Series Editors
Craig G. Bartholomew &
David J. H. Beldman

LEXHAM PRESS

Living in God's True Story: 2 Peter
Transformative Word

Copyright 2021 Donald L. Morcom

Lexham Press, 1313 Commercial St., Bellingham, WA 98225
LexhamPress.com

You may use brief quotations from this resource in presentations, articles, and books. For all other uses, please write Lexham Press for permission. Email us at permissions@lexhampress.com.

Unless otherwise indicated, Scripture quotations are taken from the Holy Bible, NEW INTERNATIONAL VERSION®, copyright © 1973, 1978, 1984, 2011 by Biblica, Inc. Used by permission. All rights reserved worldwide.

Print ISBN 9781683594833
Digital ISBN 9781683594840
Library of Congress Control Number 2021930745

Series Editors: Craig G. Bartholomew and David J. H. Beldman
Lexham Editorial: David Bomar, Claire Brubaker, Mandi Newell, and
    Danielle Thevenaz
Cover Design: Peter Park
Typesetting: Fanny Palacios

*To Jackie, faithful life companion,
who models so many of the qualities
commended in 2 Peter*

TABLE OF CONTENTS

1: Introduction 1

2: "How Firm a Foundation" 11

3: Building on the Foundation..................................... 23

4: But How Firm Is This Foundation, Really? 41

5: Looking Out for False Teachers 53

6: Resisting Scoffers 67

7: Living in Light of the End 77

Conclusion 88

Appendix: Critical Issues in Studying 2 Peter............. 91

Recommended Reading 99

Notes 101

INTRODUCTION

Which Story?

All of us live our lives according to a particular story that helps us make sense of the world and our experiences in it, and molds our attitudes and behaviors accordingly. Who am I? Why am I here? Where am I going? What should I do? Our answers to such questions reflect the story we live by. British missionary-theologian Lesslie Newbigin put it like this: "The way we understand human life depends on what conception we have of the human story. *What is the real story of which my life is a part?*"[1]

Newbigin's question is urgent because "today, as in the ancient era, the Church is confronted by a host of master narratives that contradict and compete with the gospel. The pressing issue is: *Who gets to narrate the world?*"[2] Which script or metanarrative or story controls the way we think about the world and our place in it? For some people, it's consumerism—earn all you can to acquire all you can for your own enjoyment and status. For others, it's getting to the top of whatever ladder appeals to them, whether corporate, academic, or sporting. For still others, it's the modern brand of fatalism proclaimed by a bumper sticker I see sometimes: "Life's a b*tch, and then you die." Becoming authentic Christ-followers involves leaving behind the stories that our world and our culture have taught us (many of which distill into the secular quest for the "big three"—money, sex, and power)[3] and embracing an altogether new story, God's story, as revealed to us in the Bible. But there are two particular difficulties we face in making this change. The first is that our culture's stories aren't easily loosened from our way of thinking when we become Christ-followers. They continue to influence us despite our new Christian identity, unrecognized and unquestioned, like barnacles stuck tight to a boat's hull beneath the waterline. The second is that discipleship (which in essence is teaching believers how to live according to this new and different story) is only rarely treated with the seriousness it deserves. The result is that many Christians and churches, like chameleons, simply blend into the surrounding culture and continue to live in accordance with the stories taught us by the world.

> "The way we understand human life depends on what conception we have of the human story. *What is the real story of which my life is a part?*"
>
> —Lesslie Newbigin

What can be done about this unfortunate situation? The answer lies in recognizing that the Bible tells us the true story of the world; it provides the authentic metanarrative by which we learn to live the new life in Christ. Living as Christ-followers means finding our place in this story and cultivating the beliefs, attitudes, and behaviors that fit within it.[4] In a nutshell, this is the aim of the Transformative Word series, of which this book is a part. The apostle Paul declares, "All Scripture is God-breathed and is useful for teaching, rebuking, correcting and training in righteousness" so that we may be "thoroughly equipped for every good work" (2 Tim 3:16–17). We could hardly find a better description of the power of Scripture to transform us than that. Since, as D. L. Moody declared, "The Bible was not given for our information but for our transformation,"[5] we'll want to make it our priority as Christ-followers to soak in this transformative word and allow it to mold and shape our lives according to the true story of the whole world—God's story. To put it differently, this is a story not just to be *believed*, but to be *enacted*.

"What Kind of People Ought You to Be?"

No less than the other books of the Bible, 2 Peter has an important role to play in reminding us what this true story is (reminding and remembering are repeated themes in 2 Peter). It also explains how we can order our lives in accordance with this true story—it provides practical, ethical answers to the rhetorical question in 2 Peter 3:11, "What kind of people ought you to be?"[6] Peter's readers were facing many of the challenges that Christ-followers experience today—the proliferation of pseudo-stories (especially by charlatans who want to make money out of their erroneous teachings), the scoffing and mockery of skeptics (in particular about the return of Jesus Christ and the threat of judgment), the defection of some who had previously seemed to be believers, a context of moral ambiguity, and so on. Such challenges were shaking the spiritual foundations of 2 Peter's readers, confusing and unsettling them. These embattled Christ-followers may well also have been enduring social and perhaps even physical persecution in isolated instances because of their faith. They needed a reminder of the true story of which they were a part. They needed to be reoriented to the truth of their identity and status in Christ. Second Peter plays a vital role in addressing these challenges—in fact, Peter is quite insistent that his main agenda is to remind his readers of this true story (2 Pet 1:12–15; 3:1). They will be in a good position to deal with the challenges they face if this story becomes—and remains—the paradigm for their lives.

International air travel has always had its stresses. Do you have your passport and the necessary visas? What if you miss your connecting flight? What if they lose your luggage? But all that fades into insignificance compared to a new player in the game over the last decade or two—security. If nothing else unsettles you as you prepare to board your plane, security will. Take off your shoes, and oh, your belt as well. Put your laptop, the content of your pockets, and your bag onto the conveyor belt for scanning. Did you remember to take your Swiss Army knife out of your carry-on luggage? Walk through the metal detector and hope the alarm doesn't sound. Get frisked by a total stranger wearing a uniform, just to make sure. Try to collect your belongings on the other side of the X-ray machine with a hundred other travelers breathing down your neck and trying to collect their belongings at the same time. And just when you think you are done, a security officer steps forward to run an explosives test on you. Now, "Enjoy your flight"—and get ready to do most of it again at customs and immigration on the other end.

General Mitchell International Airport in Milwaukee, Wisconsin, understands your stress. As you emerge, frazzled and disoriented, from the Concourse C security checkpoint, right in front of you is a large sign that says, "Recombobulation Area."[7] Apparently the idea of a recombobulation area began as a bit of a joke on the part of the airport staff. But it quickly caught on because weary, harried, stressed, discombobulated travelers need a space to take a few deep breaths, gather their thoughts, and begin to get on with real life once more. For the last several hours, they have had an abnormal story imposed on them: "You are a security risk, and we are going to do all we can to expose you." Perhaps they have even begun to believe this. The recombobulation area gives them the space they need to begin reorienting their lives to normality.

It's helpful to think of 2 Peter as a recombobulation area for Christ-followers whose lives have been thrown into disarray by the pressures of living in an antagonistic, skeptical, and morally confusing world. Here in 2 Peter we will (re)discover our true identity in Christ, what authentic Christian discipleship looks like, how to recognize and resist false teaching, the Christian's true hope for the future, and much more. In brief, 2 Peter is a valuable primer on the sort of people we ought to be as Christ-followers.

Why 2 Peter?

For many readers, however, 2 Peter is about the *least* likely candidate among the New Testament documents to provide any credible guidance to Christ-followers about the true story of the whole world and, consequently, the sort of people we should be as we live out this story. Second Peter is one of a small group of brief letters tucked away toward the end of the New Testament collectively called the "general" or "catholic" (universal) letters: James, 1–2 Peter, 1–3 John, and Jude. They are called "general" because they are addressed to a general readership rather than to a specific church (such as the one at Corinth) or to an individual (such as Philemon). In contrast to the intriguing story of Jesus in the Gospels, the pulsating narrative of the geographical and cultural expansion of the earliest church in Acts, the infinitely engaging and theologically rich letters of Paul, and the dramatic vision given to John in the Revelation, these General Letters can appear lightweight and inconsequential, and thus have suffered from comparative neglect both in the church and in the academy. Peter Davids laments, "While there have always been commentaries written on 2 Peter, it almost seems that the only reason was that no commentary set would be complete without such a work."[8]

Over the last decade or two, interest in the General Letters has picked up somewhat,[9] but 2 Peter (and Jude) mostly remain neglected at the margins. When last did you hear a sermon from 2 Peter? It is a short and comparatively inconspicuous letter. Furthermore, persistent questions have been raised by scholars about the authorship, dating, content, and historical reception of 2 Peter.[10] We should certainly not brush these questions under the rug, but at the same time we should not allow these concerns to obscure the valuable contribution that 2 Peter makes to our understanding of the sort of people we should be as Christ-followers. As Darian Lockett remarks,

> It is important to note that the letter calls for virtuous living in light of Jesus' provision of every need, especially in the context of the promise of and argument for the return of Christ. Both of these short and sharply composed letters [2 Peter and Jude] bear a positive charge for their first readers to live faithfully in the midst of doubt and moral ambiguity in the pluralistic context of early Christianity.[11]

And so I invite you to join me in journeying through this brief but important letter we call 2 Peter. Because it is so short (only three chapters), you can read it through from beginning to end in just a few minutes. I encourage you to do exactly this before you go any further. The brevity of 2 Peter also makes it comparatively easy to identify its main themes and get a good grip of its contents—even if scholars can spend a lifetime studying it without fully plumbing its depths. Make a point of trying to understand how every section of 2 Peter provides part of the answer to the question in 2 Peter 3:11, "What kind of people ought you to be?" Rather than trying to master 2 Peter, I invite you to let this transformative word of 2 Peter master you. Or, as Joel Green puts it, "The work of scriptural reading is not about transforming an ancient message into a modern application but the transformation of our lives though Scripture. The Bible does not present us with texts to be mastered, then, but with a word intent on shaping our lives, on mastering us."[12]

> "The letter calls for virtuous living in light of Jesus' provision of every need, especially in the context of the promise of and argument for the return of Christ"
>
> —Darian Lockett, *Introduction to the Catholic Epistles*

I'll be deeply grateful if this brief guide helps to show how 2 Peter can contribute to transforming our lives in ways that honor and glorify God.

Second Peter: An Outline

Here's a suggested outline of 2 Peter (corresponding to the chapter headings in this book) that focuses on the ways in which the letter answers the key question of 3:11, "What kind of people ought you to be?" In other words, what does a Christ-transformed life actually look like?

> **OUTLINE OF 2 PETER**
>
> 1:1–4 "How Firm a Foundation"
>
> > *What kind of people ought you to be?* People who understand and are confident about the solid foundation God has laid for them in Christ.

1:5–11 Building on the Foundation

What kind of people ought you to be?
People who are committed to building on the solid foundation laid for them in Christ, thus becoming fruitful and effective in the Christian life, and confirming God's calling and choice of them.

1:12–21 How Firm Is This Foundation, Really?

What kind of people ought you to be?
People who are confident that the gospel message they have believed has come from God-directed prophets and from apostles who were eyewitnesses of the power and coming of the Lord Jesus Christ.

2:1–22 Looking Out for False Teachers

What kind of people ought you to be?
People who are alert to false teachers who promise the world but in reality want to mislead and exploit them.

3:1–10 Resisting Scoffers

What kind of people ought you to be?
People who stand up against skeptics who deny the second coming of Christ and the coming judgment.

3:11–18 Living in Light of the End

What kind of people ought you to be?
People who are eagerly looking forward to the coming day of the Lord, and who are living holy and godly lives in anticipation of it.

SUGGESTED READING

☐ All of 2 Peter, preferably in one sitting

Reflection

What is the value of understanding our lives in terms of a controlling worldview, or metanarrative, or story of which we are part?

_____

_____

_____

Think about the society or culture of which you are part. What are some of the controlling stories that determine how people live in your context? How do you see these stories playing out in popular beliefs and patterns of behavior?

_____

_____

_____

Based on your reading of 2 Peter, how does the idea of competing stories or metanarratives help us to understand its main message?

_____

_____

_____

"HOW FIRM A FOUNDATION"

2 PETER 1:1–4

In my home country of Australia, as in many other parts of the world, termites—"white ants," as we call them here— pose a significant threat to wooden structures. White ants are only small creatures, but they can do an awful lot of damage. Unseen and unnoticed, they eat away at house frames, floors, posts, fences, and anything else made of wood that they can sink their teeth into. You have no idea that anything is wrong until one day you lean unsuspectingly against a wall and it suddenly gives way. Prevention is better than cure, of course—most Aussie homeowners spend plenty of good money to keep the white ants at bay and the pest-control industry in business. So pervasive are white ants that their name features in the vocabulary of politics and organizational life—to "white-ant" a political party or an organization is to undermine or sabotage it.

Peter makes it clear that false teachers and scoffers were trying to "white-ant" the faith of his readers (see especially 2 Pet 2:1–3:7), so it makes sense that Peter would be at pains to remind them of the solid, white ant-proof foundation that God has already laid for them in Christ. When we try to answer the transformative question of 2 Peter 3:11, "What kind of people ought you to be?" we must begin with a clear understanding of this unshakable foundation. For our encouragement and assurance, Peter sets out the security and benefits of belonging to God and being part of his true story in the introduction to his letter (1:1–4).

A Greeting from the Author

As is customary in many of the letters of the New Testament, the author begins by identifying himself. He is "Simeon Peter, a slave and apostle of Jesus Christ" (2 Pet 1:1, my translation).[13] The longer version of his name, "Simeon," is found only here and in Acts 15:14, where James refers to him in this way at the Jerusalem Council. "Simeon" is the transliteration of the Hebrew name of the son of Jacob and the tribe named after him in the Old Testament; "Simon" is the common Greek form of his name, and many English translations opt for this rendering.

Simon Peter was one of the first disciples called to follow Jesus (Matt 4:18–20; Luke 5:1–11). He stands out in the Gospels as the leader of the disciples and someone capable of passionate affirmations of the true identity of Jesus as Messiah (see Matt 16:16–18, the occasion when Jesus gives him his new name, "Peter"; John 6:66–69). With James and John, he was also a member of the inner circle, whom Jesus involved at key points in his ministry, such as the raising of Jairus' daughter (Mark 5:37; Luke 8:51) and the transfiguration (Matt 17:1-9; Mark 9:1-9; Luke 9:27-36), an event Peter recalls in 2 Peter 1:16-18. But he was also impetuous and guilty of some disappointing failures, the worst being his denial of Jesus (Matt 26:69-75; Mark 14:66-72; Luke 22:54-62; John 18:15-27). As he was shattered by guilt at his failure, his reinstatement by Jesus in John 21:15-19 marks a turning point in his life that he never forgot. The two letters that bear his name, 1 and 2 Peter, are part of his obedient response to commands he received directly from Jesus: "And when you have turned back, strengthen your brothers" (Luke 22:32), and "Feed my lambs. ... Feed my sheep" (John 21:15, 17).

Empowered by the Holy Spirit following the day of Pentecost, at which he preached a crucial sermon (Acts 2:14-36), Peter became an important figure in the geographical and cultural spread of the gospel in Acts. Although Galatians 2:7-9 describes a division of labor— Paul to the gentiles, and Peter (Cephas) to the Jews—this division was not completely watertight. Even if his practice sometimes lagged behind his theology (Gal 2:11-14), Peter was instrumental in the earliest stages of preaching the gospel to the gentiles. His vision at Joppa led to his proclaiming the gospel to the Roman centurion Cornelius and his household (Acts 10:1-11:18). After his miraculous, angel-enabled escape from prison, Peter "left for another place" (Acts 12:17)—unspecified, but probably well outside the Jewish orbit, in which his life was now threatened. He reappeared to make a convincing speech at the Jerusalem Council (Acts 15:6-11), which paved the way for the decision *not* to "make it difficult for the Gentiles who are turning to God" (Acts 15:19) by adding the weight of observing Jewish ceremonial law. After this, we know very little about Peter's own personal history. He addresses his first letter to "God's elect, exiles scattered throughout the provinces of Pontus, Galatia, Cappadocia, Asia and Bithynia" (1 Pet 1:1), an area covering much of the western half of modern Turkey, suggesting that he had significant influence there. According to early Christian testimony, Peter met martyrdom in Rome by being crucified head down during the reign of the emperor Nero (reigned AD 54–68) in the mid-60s AD.[14]

Peter further identifies himself as "a slave and apostle of Jesus Christ" (2 Pet 1:1, my translation). For good reasons, many people today recoil from the use of the word "slave" to describe a Christian's relationship with Christ. You can easily understand why if you have seen uncomfortable but important movies such as *Amistad* or *Twelve Years a Slave*, where the horrors of slavery are vividly depicted.[15] Many English versions of the New Testament (KJV, NIV, ESV) soften the translation of the Greek word *doulos* to "servant" or "bondservant" (the former is too weak, and the latter too archaic, to do justice to *doulos*), but they show little hesitation in referring to the false teachers as "slaves" of corruption (2 Pet 2:19, where the same word *doulos* is used). We need to understand that for New Testament writers such as Peter and Paul, *doulos* carries the idea of a completely sold-out commitment to Jesus Christ and the mission he had given them—the apostolic mission of taking the true story of the gospel to their world. There is really no other way of understanding their—and our—Christian identity.

By referring to himself as an "apostle," Peter is claiming the right to speak with authority to his readers, since he had been appointed by Jesus Christ himself for this task. But at the same time, Peter wants to make sure that his readers understand that they are not in any sense inferior to the apostles as far as their faith is concerned—in fact, God has chosen them to receive "a faith as precious" (2 Pet 1:1) as the apostles' faith. The same "righteousness of our God and Savior Jesus Christ" (2 Pet 1:1) that was at work in the apostles is also at work in Peter's believing readers.[16] There are no second-class citizens among God's people.

> For New Testament writers such as Peter and Paul, the Greek word *doulos* ("servant") carries the idea of a completely sold-out commitment to Jesus Christ.

A Foundation Laid by God

"Grace and peace be yours" (2 Pet 1:2) is a characteristically Christian greeting in the New Testament—variations of it appear at the beginning of every one of Paul's letters, plus 1 and 2 Peter, 2 John, and Revelation. The grace of God and peace with God encapsulate both the ground of our salvation and its most important result. It's no wonder that Peter expresses the longing that grace and peace may be multiplied to his readers, because these are among the most important and valuable benefits of knowing Jesus Christ and are the most important ingredients of the solid foundation on which we stand. Grace, peace, and knowing Jesus Christ are vital as our spiritual foundation, which Peter demonstrates by using them as inclusive bookends to his letter (compare 2 Pet 1:2 with 3:14, 18).

Here's the crucially important point: no one less than God himself has laid the foundation on which believers stand. As Christ-followers, this is the source of our confidence and assurance. *God* takes the initiative in our salvation; *God* lays the foundation on which our Christian lives are built. This point is made repeatedly in the New Testament (for example, Rom 3:21–26; 1 Cor 1:26–31; Eph 2:8–9; Phil 3:9; 2 Tim 1:9; Titus 3:5), because it is vital for Christ-followers to understand that the righteousness of Jesus Christ, our God and Savior, is the basis and foundation of our salvation, *not* our own righteousness. Peter establishes this indispensable principle at the very beginning of his letter. "*His* divine power" (2 Pet 1:3) has bestowed on us everything that contributes to life and godliness; *he* is the one who has called us to his own glory and goodness (1:3); *he* is the one who has made us the objects of his great and precious promises (1:4).

> No one less than God himself has laid the foundation on which believers stand.

I still remember quite vividly as a young teenager being let down by someone who had committed to doing something and failed to carry through on that commitment. "But you promised to do it!" I said. "No," was the response, "I didn't *promise* I'd do it, I only *said* I would." As if there were a difference! Thankfully, God's character is the guarantee that he will keep his promises. As Paul declares so confidently, "For no matter how many promises God has made, they are 'Yes' in Christ" (2 Cor 1:20). (At the same time, of course, we need to be more careful than we often are about interpreting God's promises *in their context*. God often gave specific promises to individuals or groups of people in specific historical circumstances that can't be extended willy-nilly to us and our circumstances.)

Here in 2 Peter, however, Peter seems to have a very specific set of promises in mind, God's promises about the future hope of Christians. Yet it is at this very point of God's promises that skeptics are leveling their attack against Peter's readers. "[Scoffers] will say, 'Where is this 'coming' he promised?'" (2 Pet 3:4). But Peter wants to reinforce his readers' assurance that "the Lord is not slow in keeping his promise" (3:9), and it is "in keeping with his promise" that Christ-followers await their glorious future, "a new heaven and a new earth, where righteousness dwells" (3:13).

Not only that, but Peter assures his readers that God has called believers to "participate in the divine nature" (2 Pet 1:4). The Greek word used here, *koinōnoi*, means "people who partake or share in something." In this context, it's important to clarify what participating in the divine nature does *not* mean. Both ancient Greek philosophy[17] and the contemporary New Age movement have suggested that humans have a "divine spark" within them and can even become gods. One website I chose at random makes this startling offer: "When you learn the Three Godlike Powers of divination, evocation and soul travel, you'll be ominiscient [sic], omnipotent, and omnipresent—literally a Living God."[18]

Of course, this is not at all what Peter has in mind when he declares that through God's promises "you may participate in the divine nature" (2 Pet 1:4). Rather than becoming God or being absorbed into God, believers are invited into the kind of fellowship with God that transforms and energizes their lives.[19] As biblical commentary on becoming partakers of the divine nature, think about Jesus' illustration of the vine and the branches (John 15:1–6), or Paul's affirmation in Galatians 2:20: "I have been crucified with Christ and I no longer live, but Christ lives in me. The life I now live in the body, I live by faith in the Son of God, who loved me and gave himself for me." The creation account in the early chapters of Genesis makes it clear that there is an eternal qualitative distinction between the Creator and the creation. Humans were never intended to become God—on the contrary, the fall happened precisely when the serpent tempted our original forebears to be "like God" (Gen 3:5). Humans were created as divine image-bearers (Gen 1:26–27), but the serpent was tempting them to become gods themselves.

When Peter speaks of our becoming partakers of the divine nature, he is saying that God offers us his own life to share. Or, as Michael Gorman puts it (in a book that is about Paul, but Peter would agree!), being partakers of the divine nature means "Spirit-enabled transformative participation in the life and character of God revealed in the crucified and resurrected Messiah Jesus."[20] I hope that you are keeping in the back of your mind Peter's question, "What kind of people ought you to be?" (2 Pet 3:11). The answer to Peter's question provided in 2 Peter 1:3–4 is this: we ought to be people through whom the love and holiness and life of God shine. We are called into fellowship with the Trinity, and as such we reflect the God-life in our own lives (Peter will show us what such a life looks like in 1:5–15). We have explicitly renounced the world's version of the story by which we ought to live our lives; as Christ-followers, we have escaped the ruin that is the destiny of those who live in obedience to their evil desires (1:4). On the contrary, as the result of the grace of God and the peace with God that we now enjoy, we have embraced the God-story as the true story of the world and of our lives.

> When Peter speaks of our becoming partakers of the divine nature, he is saying that God offers us his own life to share.

But Is 2 Peter Really about the Gospel?

An objection raised against the value of 2 Peter is the alleged absence of the gospel from it. You'll look in vain for any overt mention of the cross of Jesus Christ or the doctrine of the atonement in 2 Peter. Compared with Romans or Galatians, for example, there is no clear presentation of the gospel message in 2 Peter. This is one of the reasons why 2 Peter has been called the "ugly stepchild" of the New Testament, or even "sub-Christian."[21] But before we jump to such conclusions, let us hear its important message and submit to its instruction, bearing two important considerations in mind.

The first consideration is that the gospel message is *assumed* in 2 Peter rather than explicitly affirmed. Clearly, Peter's readers are already believers in Jesus Christ. The rich language of 2 Peter 1:1–4 leaves us in no doubt about this: they have been chosen to receive a faith equally precious to that of the apostles (1:1); they have received their right standing with God "through the righteousness of our God and Savior Jesus Christ" (1:1); they have come to experience the grace of God and peace with God as a result of their personal knowledge of God and of the Lord Jesus (1:2); through knowing him and experiencing his own power in their lives, they are the recipients of everything they need for life and godliness (1:3); they have been called by God into relationship with him (1:3); they are the objects of God's wonderful promises to give them a share in his own life (1:4); and they have escaped from the corruption that is in the world (1:4). Far from being in tension with Paul, Peter specifically affirms the message of salvation that is so prominent in Paul's letters (3:15–16). The gospel is a given in 2 Peter, and Peter's readers have already received it with open arms.

But for whatever reason (perhaps largely due to the activities of the false teachers and scoffers who are described in 2 Pet 2:1–3:7), Peter's readers seem to have stalled in their Christian development. This is the second consideration—Peter's aim in this letter is to enable his readers to live faithfully in light of the gospel that they have already received. In other words, 2 Peter is less concerned about *coming* to faith (important though that is to Peter) than it is about *growing* in faith. For Peter and the other writers of the New Testament documents, there is no such thing as "easy believism"—no "walk the aisle and you're in" decisionism. The gospel is meant to make a profound and radical difference to the way we live. So, for example, Peter is insistent in his reminders to them to "add" Christian virtues to their faith (1:5-7), to "increase" in such qualities (1:8), and to "grow" in grace and in their knowledge of their Lord and Savior Jesus Christ (3:18).

> Second Peter is less concerned about *coming* to faith than it is about *growing* in faith.

How should we build on the foundation that God has laid through our Lord and Savior Jesus Christ? Or, in terms of Peter's question that we are using to help organize our approach to his letter, what sort of people should we be (2 Pet 3:11) in light of the firm gospel foundation that God has already laid in our lives? These are vitally important questions to which 2 Peter provides a rich and variegated answer, as we shall see.

SUGGESTED READING

☐ 2 Peter 1:1–4

☐ John 21

☐ Ephesians 1

Reflection

In 2 Peter 1:1, Peter describes himself as a *doulos* (variously translated "slave" or "servant") and apostle of Jesus Christ. What are the strengths and weaknesses of understanding Peter's (and our) relationship to Jesus Christ as his "slaves" or "servants"? What difference does it make?

_____

_____

_____

Working from 2 Peter 1:1–4, make a list of the roles of "God and of Jesus our Lord" (v. 2) in our salvation. In what ways should this be an encouragement to us?

_____

_____

_____

I suggested that "2 Peter is less concerned about *coming* to faith than it is about *growing* in faith." How should this awareness affect our approach to the book, especially for those concerned that 2 Peter doesn't deal sufficiently with the gospel?

_____

_____

_____

3

BUILDING ON THE FOUNDATION

2 PETER 1:5–11

I used to drive past a prime piece of real estate in a light industrial area almost every day, wondering why it had never been built on. Then one day the heavy machinery arrived, excavations began, and foundations were laid. And nothing further happened! This is not what completed foundations are for. For a long time, the site lay unattended and neglected, and weeds grew in abundance. I wondered whether perhaps a business deal had turned sour, or the owners had gone bankrupt. At last, after some years, work began again, and now a striking modern building stands proudly on the site. Foundations are *meant* to be built on. By themselves they don't serve much purpose, but they provide the indispensable strength and stability when something is built on them. The wise man in Jesus' parable about the importance of building on the rock (Matt 7:24–27) understood this principle very well.

And so did Peter. He has already reminded his believing readers of the solid foundation God has laid for them in Christ (2 Pet 1:1–4). Now he urges them to build on this foundation the kind of life and character that will make them effective and fruitful as Christ-followers (1:8) and will assure them of a warm welcome into the eternal kingdom of their Lord and Savior Jesus Christ (1:11).

Building Christian Character

To understand Peter's emphasis on building on the foundation that God has laid in our lives (and also to dispel the notion of tensions between Paul and Peter on this point), recall Paul's affirmation in 1 Corinthians 3:11–13:

> For no one can lay any foundation other than the one already laid, which is Jesus Christ. If anyone builds on this foundation using gold, silver, costly stones, wood, hay or straw, their work will be shown for what it is, because the Day will bring it to light. It will be revealed with fire, and the fire will test the quality of each person's work.

Peter and Paul both affirm that God has laid the foundation for the Christian life, and they both affirm the need for Christ-followers to build on that foundation. Implicit in Paul's appeal is the call to build with high-quality materials—gold, silver, costly stones—and to avoid substandard materials that won't survive the fires of judgment. The agenda of 2 Peter is much the same.

> Peter and Paul both affirm that God has laid the
> foundation for the Christian life, and they both
> affirm the need for Christ-followers to build on
> that foundation.

Martin Luther, the great German Reformer of the early sixteenth century, is justifiably famous for his rediscovery of the doctrine of justification by faith, as against the prevailing ideas of works-based righteousness in the late medieval church. Two of his famous *Ninety-Five Theses* (1517), the work that sparked the German Reformation of the sixteenth century, read as follows:

> 25. The one who does much "work" is not
> the righteous one, but the one who, without
> "work," has much faith in Christ.
>
> 26. The law says: "Do this!", and it never is
> done. Grace says, "Believe in this one!," and
> forthwith everything is done.[22]

After Luther's death in 1546, there was a succession dispute for the leadership of German Protestantism. One party, the so-called Gnesio-Lutherans (or "pure Lutherans"), trying to be faithful to their understanding of Luther's teaching, argued that salvation was by grace through faith alone to the extent that good works could actually endanger one's salvation. Salvation is God's work alone; any admixture of works undermines this doctrine. Viewed in this light, you can understand the caution of Luther and his Gnesio-Lutheran followers about the value of the letter of James, which Luther regarded as "an epistle of straw," owing to statements such as "faith by itself, if it is not accompanied by action, is dead" (Jas 2:17). Second Peter was tarred with much the same brush—the notion of adding anything to one's faith seemed to be a denial of the Reformation doctrine of *sola fide* (by faith alone). Monergism (the teaching that salvation is the work of God alone) needed to be protected against synergism (the notion that humans cooperate with God in some way to attain salvation).

But making a dichotomy between faith and works is a misunderstanding of what Peter is saying (not to mention James and Paul). They agree that the salvation-foundation is God's work alone, but they are also concerned with how believers build on this foundation. As Michael Horton puts it, "Grace is not opposed to human activity. It's opposed to human merit."[23] The notion of a Christian who does not display the fruits of Christian character would have been inconceivable to New Testament writers such as Peter. Now that believers have escaped from the ruin that is in the world because of unbridled desire (2 Pet 1:4), it is unthinkable that they should go on living as before. Works issue from faith and are its necessary consequence. Sanctification flows from justification. For the very reason (1:5) that God has laid this foundation in our lives and given us all we need for living a godly life (1:3), we must do our utmost to build responsibly on it.

For many people raised in a Christian context, this all seems pretty obvious. But it was not obvious to converts from pagan backgrounds (as many of Peter's readers would have been), just as it is not obvious today to people who come to Christ from secular backgrounds. In countries that were once part of "the Christian West" (including my own, Australia) and others where Christianity is largely unknown, many people who become believers in Christ have no Christian background whatever. Hence the need to provide such converts with instruction not just about Christian *teaching* but also about Christian *living*. This is a vital theme in 2 Peter—teaching readers what it means to be intentional about living the true story of the whole world and leaving them with no doubt about the sort of people we should be.

Other early Christian writings take up the same theme. One example is the Didache (the full title is The Teaching of the Lord to the Gentiles by the Twelve Apostles), dating perhaps from the late first or early second century. Its purpose is to prepare new converts for baptism and membership in the church. "There are two ways," the Didache begins, "one of life and one of death, and there is a great difference between these two ways."[24] It then goes on to describe these two ways in detail, providing clear instruction of the sort of behavior required in the Christian way of life as contrasted with the preconversion way of death. In a similar vein, as part of his answer to the transformative question, "What kind of people ought you to be?" (2 Pet 3:11), Peter provides a list of qualities we need to cultivate as Christians (1:5-7).

A Catalog of Christian Virtues

Peter uses forceful language to introduce his list of Christian character qualities: "make every effort" (2 Pet 1:5). The same urgency is reflected in 1:10, 15; 3:14—

reminders that being Christ-followers involves passionate and ongoing effort to cultivate Christian character and behavior. Don Carson explains:

> People do not drift toward holiness. Apart from grace-driven effort, people do not gravitate toward godliness, prayer, obedience to Scripture, faith, and delight in the Lord. We drift toward compromise and call it tolerance; we drift toward disobedience and call it freedom; we drift toward superstition and call it faith. We cherish the indiscipline of lost self-control and call it relaxation; we slouch toward prayerlessness and delude ourselves into thinking we have escaped legalism; we slide toward godlessness and convince ourselves we have been liberated.[25]

It is worth making the point again: 2 Peter is less concerned about *coming* to faith (that foundation is assumed) and more about *growing* in faith—which here involves adding to our faith-commitment the "chain of virtues"[26] in 2 Peter 1:5–7.

There are several such lists of Christian character qualities in the New Testament (for example, Rom 5:3–5; Jas 1:3–4; and the fruit of the Spirit in Gal 5:22–23). While the lists in Romans and James are clearly progressive, this doesn't appear to be the case with Peter's list. It borrows some qualities familiar to readers from a Jewish or Greek cultural background but adds some distinctively Christian qualities. Not that there is anything wrong with cultivating appropriate virtues borrowed from society: "The borrowings testify to the fact that Christian ethics cannot be discontinuous with the moral ideals of non-Christian society, but the new context in which they are set ensures that they are subordinated to and to be interpreted by reference to the central Christian principle of love."[27] Peter's list comprises seven character qualities he urges his readers to add to the faith-foundation already laid in their lives. Think of a choir or an orchestra *adding* to the melody extra harmonious parts to create a rich and beautiful sound.[28]

> Peter's list comprises seven character qualities he urges his readers to add to the faith-foundation already laid in their lives.

Goodness (*aretē*)

Goodness, or virtue, is the character trait of moral excellence or uprightness.[29] Christians should have a reputation for "excellence of character"[30] and for being the finest of citizens. We should be the exact opposite of the false teachers whose behavior "will bring the way of truth into disrepute" (2 Pet 2:2; see also Rom 2:24). In Australia, a Royal Commission into Institutional Responses to Child Sexual Abuse has recently completed its work. Sadly, a number of church groups were implicated. Not only were children sexually abused within these church groups, but there were systematic cover-ups of the abuses and exoneration of the perpetrators. Such deplorable behavior is the exact opposite of the "goodness" to which Peter calls Christian believers.

Knowledge (gnōsis)

In 2 Peter two Greek words are translated "knowledge." Although their meanings overlap to a degree, the word used here (gnōsis) focuses on the accumulation of true factual knowledge about Jesus Christ and the Christian faith (the same word is also used in 3:18). Peter is at pains to stress the importance of such knowledge in 2 Peter 1:16–21 as an antidote to the erroneous ideas being peddled by the false teachers and scoffers (2 Pet 2:1–3:7; see Eph 4:13–14). Ignorance may be bliss, but it has no place in the Christian life. The other word in 2 Peter translated "knowledge" (epignōsis) slants more in the direction of personal or experiential knowledge (2 Pet 1:2, 3, 8; 2:20). While there is obviously a close connection between the two words, and both kinds of knowledge are clearly indispensable, knowledge here is "the wisdom and discernment which the Christian needs for a virtuous life and which is progressively acquired. It is practical rather than purely speculative wisdom (cf. Phil 1:9)."[31]

Self-Control (enkrateia)

Self-control means channeling our desires and passions into God-honoring behavior. Of course, this does not mean that desire is wrong as such. For example, sexual desire is a gift from God, but it is intended to be used within the proper boundaries of marriage. The Greek philosopher Socrates remarked, "Should not every man hold self-control to be the foundation of all virtue, and first lay this foundation firmly in his soul? For who without this can learn any good or practice it worthily?"[32] To any musician or athlete, this will make perfect sense. There are always a million and one more pleasurable and entic-ing things to do than the endless practice and training necessary to play in a symphony orchestra or be part of a premier-grade sports team, but you need the discipline of self-control to lay aside such temptations if you are going develop the needed skills. How much more important is self-control in the Christian life?

Paul too picks up on precisely this point: "Everyone who competes in the games goes into strict training. They do it to get a crown that will not last, but we do it to get a crown that will last forever" (1 Cor 9:25). Peter has already hinted at the importance of self-control in the Christian life by contrasting our previous lives in the world, which were driven by uncontrolled desire or lust (2 Pet 1:4), and the greed that drives the false teachers (2 Pet 2:3, 14, 18). Once we lived that way (see 1 Pet 4:1–5), but no more!

Perseverance (*hypomonē*)

As a one-time marathon runner, the pinnacle of my very modest achievements was completing the eighty-nine kilometer (fifty-five mile) Comrades Marathon in South Africa three times. There were always runners complain-ing that it was too hot or too cold, that there was too much wind or not enough breeze, that it was too rainy or too dry. We were coached to forget about adverse conditions, put our heads down, and get the job done. In a marathon, both good and bad patches come and go. For back-of-the-pack plodders like me, the cardinal rule was, "Keep moving forward!"

The Christian life is a marathon, not a sprint. It is a race to be run with perseverance and endurance, or what my dad used to call "stickability" (Heb 12:1; see also Jas 1:3-4 and Rom 5:3-5, where the same word, *hypomonē*, is used). In a marathon, especially when you are going through a bad patch, the thought of crossing the finishing line and getting a medal motivates you to persevere. The antidote to flagging spirits in the marathon of the Christian life is the hope promised to us as Christ-followers (2 Pet 1:11; 3:13; 1 Pet 1:3-5; Phil 3:13-14). The anticipation of the Lord's "Well done, good and faithful servant!" (Matt 25:21, 23; Luke 19:17) boosts our ability to persevere in difficult times. Yet we are not left to our own strength and devices when it comes to persevering as Christians in difficult times and challenging circumstances. Recall the assurance that "[God's] divine power has given us everything we need for a godly life" and that "he has given us his very great and precious promises" (2 Pet 1:3-4).

Godliness (*eusebeia*)

If God has given us "everything we need for a godly life" (2 Pet 1:3), and if we should be people characterized by "holy and godly lives" (3:11), it is no surprise that godliness should be part of the chain of virtues that Peter urges us to cultivate. In the world of Peter's first readers, *eusebeia* was mostly understood as reverence and loyalty. Here in 2 Peter "the virtue points up the necessity of loyalty to God and to the community in which the readers are embedded."[33] The way to demonstrate loyalty to God and his people is ordering our lives in a way that reflects God's holy character and strengthens the believing community.

Mutual Affection (*philadelphia*)

The focus remains on the believing community as Peter urges his readers to cultivate *philadelphia*, literally, care, affection, or love for one's own siblings. Blood, as the saying goes, is thicker than water. In the New Testament, the term *philadelphia* appears only rarely (twice here in 2 Pet 1:7; 1 Pet 1:22; Rom 12:10; 1 Thess 4:9; Heb 13:1), but in each of these instances love or affection for those who are our brothers and sisters in the Christian faith is in mind. We are all saved into a family (the people of God, the body of Christ, the church). This new family, which takes precedence over even our blood family (Mark 3:31-35), is the context in which we are called to live and practice the Christian life. It is simply not possible to practice *philadelphia* by yourself! Many churches in the Western world, afflicted as they are by an individualist mentality, need to recover a sense of family and community.

Love (*agapē*)

Christian love (*agapē*) is the fitting climax to Peter's list and must be the most prominent and recognizable feature of the Christian life (Col 3:14; 1 Thess 3:12-13; 1 Pet 1:22). In contemporary English usage, however, the word "love" has taken on many different shades of meaning, some leading away from rather than toward a biblical understanding of the term. Part of understanding the new, true story of the world—God's story—and conforming our lives to it is learning the meaning of *agapē* love according to this new story. Here description is probably better than definition, and there is no better description of *agapē* love in the New Testament than in 1 Corinthians 13. "The important point to keep in mind," writes Peter Davids, "is that love is a virtue, not an emotion. Christians are not encouraged to feel warmly about each other or even to like one another; they are instructed to act lovingly toward one another. Thus Paul's description of love in 1 Corinthians 13 speaks about what love does, how it acts, not how it feels."[34] An old Don Francisco song rightly reminds us, "Love is not a feeling, it's an act of your will."[35]

Cultivating the Christian Virtues

If this list of Christian character qualities in 2 Peter 1:5–7 is a portrait of the sort of people we should be as Christ-followers, what practical steps can we take to integrate them into our lives? Here are some suggestions.

1.   Take seriously the affirmation that God's divine power has given us everything we need for a godly life (2 Pet 1:3). He has not left us to our own devices in cultivating Christian character; he is an active partner with us in this endeavor. Paul puts it like this: "Continue to work out your own salvation with fear and trembling, for it is God who works in you to will and to act in order to fulfill his good purpose" (Phil 2:12b–13). Make a sincere prayer of your desire to cooperate with him in developing these qualities.

2.   Make this journey of transformation in company with other members of the body of Christ. The Christian journey toward character

transformation and Christlikeness is *meant* to be made in the company of other believers. Make yourself accountable to a small group of trusted, like-minded believers to build these qualities into your life. Seek out Christians in your faith community who exemplify these qualities and ask to be mentored by them. Your faith community also provides an ideal environment for exercising these qualities as you grow in them.

3. Read good Christian biography and autobiography. Here is an opportunity to meet firsthand some of the finest Christians who have ever lived and to find out what made them tick. The stories of faithful people such as Augustine, Corrie ten Boom, Elisabeth Elliot, John Newton, and many others will inspire you in the area of Christian virtue. Google "best Christian biography" and you'll find several sites to point you in the right direction.[36]

4. Make a character study of biblical heroes of faith. The catalog in Hebrews 11 is a good place to start. When all is said and done, however, it is the character of Jesus Christ himself that best encapsulates all of the qualities in Peter's list. The fifteenth-century author of *The Imitation of Christ*, Thomas à Kempis, wrote: "We should imitate [Christ's] life and manners if we want to be truly enlightened and delivered from all blindness of heart. Let our chief endeavor, therefore, be to meditate on the life of Jesus Christ."[37]

God's ultimate goal for our lives as Christians is for us to be conformed to the image of his Son (Rom 8:29).

Avoiding Spiritual Myopia and Amnesia

Regardless of the importance and intrinsic value of cultivating the Christian character qualities in Peter's list, we should not think of them as ends in themselves. Rather, they are means toward the end of greater usefulness in the Christian life. Literally, they keep us from being "do-nothings" and "fruitless" as we grow into knowing our Lord Jesus Christ better and better (2 Pet 1:8). Idleness and fruitlessness have no place in the lives of believers. Once again, we find Peter and Paul in agreement—Paul reminds the Thessalonians, "We instructed you how to live in order to please God, as in fact you are living. Now we ask and urge you in the Lord Jesus to do this more and more" (1 Thess 4:1).

> Peter labels the failure to cultivate these virtues as forgetfulness, nearsightedness, and blindness.

Jesus too emphasized the importance of fruitfulness and good stewardship on numerous occasions. Recall, for example, the parable of the sower (Matt 13:1–23): "But the seed falling on good soil refers to someone who hears the word and understands it. This is the one who produces a crop, yielding a hundred, sixty or thirty times what was sown" (Matt 13:23). Ponder Jesus' imagery of the vine and the branches, and the need for fruitfulness (John 15:1–8).

Let yourself be confronted again by the challenge of parables that highlight the responsible use of the investment our master has made in our lives (Matt 25:14–30; Luke 19:11–27).

Just as a healthy, vigorously growing lawn is the best protection against getting weeds in that lawn, so too a life committed to the cultivation of the Christian character virtues is the best protection against being ineffective and unproductive in our Christian lives. By way of contrast, Peter labels the failure to cultivate these virtues as forgetfulness, nearsightedness, and blindness (2 Pet 1:9). It is to lapse into the old pseudo-stories that governed our lives before we came to know Jesus Christ and to experience his forgiveness. It is building with wood, hay, and straw, which the false teachers and scoffers (2 Pet 2:1–3:7), like big bad wolves, will be able to blow away with ease. Failing to understand our Christian status and responsibility clearly is a tragedy that Peter will do his utmost to help us avoid.

Confirm Your Calling and Election

In 2 Peter 1:10, Peter again urges his readers to "make every effort" to do something (we have noticed this in 1:5; it will recur in 3:14). There are to be no half-measures—Christ-followers should be every bit as committed to cultivating their Christian identity and practice as elite athletes are to their training and nutrition programs. This time, the instruction is "to confirm your calling and election" (2 Pet 1:10). There's a certain amount of shock value in this command—how can we make our calling and election sure, since it is clearly God who calls and chooses us? Conscious of the apparent theological awkwardness of such a command, the NASB renders it like this: "Be all the more diligent to make certain about His calling and choosing you." But this weakens the force of what Peter is saying.

One of my colleagues, Ian Hussey, recently completed a research degree that examined the use of the term "call" in Luke and Paul. He demonstrated clearly that calling links in very closely with God's summons to us to salvation, represented graphically in the imagery of the invitations to the great banquet (Luke 14:15–23). The problem in that parable was that the invited guests neglected to confirm their calling or invitation by failing to show up at the banquet and making all kinds of excuses instead. Conversely, the nobodies in the streets and alleys and country lanes were offered the opportunity to make their unanticipated calling and choice sure by actually arriving (some even under compulsion) at the banquet.

> The cultivation of these virtues is our acceptance of the invitation (or activation of it, if you like); this is how we ratify God's calling and choice of us.

In the wider context of 2 Peter 1, it is abundantly clear that God is the one who provides salvation to us. It is *his* righteousness that confers faith on us (2 Pet 1:1); it is *his* divine power that has given us everything we need for a godly life (2 Pet 1:3). And yet we are commanded to add to this faith foundation the virtues listed in 2 Peter 1:5–7.

The cultivation of these virtues is our acceptance of the invitation (or activation of it, if you like); this is how we ratify God's calling and choice of us. Confirmation of the imagery comes in 2 Peter 1:11: the word translated "rich welcome" (*eisodos*) focuses on the orchestration of an appropriate reception—a lavish welcome to us as we arrive as guests of honor to take our undeserved place in the eternal kingdom of our Lord and Savior, Jesus Christ.

SUGGESTED READING

☐ 2 Peter 1:5–11

☐ Matthew 7:24–27

☐ 1 Corinthians 3:10–15

Reflection

Compare the "fruit of the Spirit" in Galatians 5:22-23 with the list of Christian virtues in 2 Peter 1:5-7. What are the similarities? The differences?

_____

_____

_____

_____

The fruit of the Spirit in Galatians 5:22–23 is clearly the result of the *Spirit's* work in the lives of believers, yet in 2 Peter 1:5–7 *believers* are exhorted to make every effort to add the virtues to their faith. How would you explain this apparent tension?

_____

_____

_____

_____

Comparing your own life to Peter's list of virtues in 2 Peter 1:5–7, where are you healthy? What areas need more work? How, practically speaking, will you seek by God's grace to cultivate these virtues?

_____

_____

_____

_____

4

BUT HOW FIRM IS THIS FOUNDATION, REALLY?

2 PETER 1:12–21

Many of the letters in the New Testament follow a recognizable pattern. First, there is a teaching section, explaining what God has done in Christ to assure our salvation. Second, there is a practical section, dealing with the appropriate response from our side. Peter follows that pattern here. First, he explains to his readers what God has done for them by way of laying the necessary foundation for the Christian life (2 Pet 1:1–4). Then, he urges them to build responsibly on this foundation (1:5–11). So far, so good.

But Peter's readers are under threat. Their Christian experience is anything but strawberries and cream. More than a third of his letter (2:1–3:7) is about false teachers and mockers who will seek to derail them from their faith and undermine their Christian confidence. Centuries earlier, the exiles who returned from Babylon soon discovered that it was one thing to rebuild the ruined walls of Jerusalem; it was quite another to do so in the face of their enemies' sustained military opposition and mockery (see the story in Neh 4). It is all very well to live an authentic Christian life under ideal circumstances. But, truthfully, circumstances are never ideal. Christ-followers perpetually live in the throes of spiritual battle (Eph 6:10–20). In the face of competing stories, is the true story of the whole world *actually* true? Will the foundation hold? How firm is it—*really?* Peter's response to these questions centers on the cultivation of a clear Christian memory about the gospel his readers have been taught, and reassurances about the certainty of the apostolic and prophetic word on which they have taken their stand.

Don't Forget to Remember!

As Middle-earth teeters on the brink of ruin at the beginning of Peter Jackson's cinematic epic *The Lord of the Rings: The Fellowship of the Ring*, viewers hear the words of Galadriel in somber voiceover: "The world is changed: I feel it in the water, I feel it in the earth, I smell it in the air. ... Much that once was is lost, for none now live who remember it. ... But the hearts of Men are easily corrupted. And the Ring of Power has a will of its own. ... And some things that should not have been forgotten ... were lost."[38]

Galadriel could easily have been describing the kind of person Peter refers to in 2 Peter 1:9—nearsighted, blind, and *forgetful:* "Much that once was is lost, for none now live who remember it. And some things that should not have been forgotten ... were lost." Think for a moment of someone with amnesia—complete memory loss. He can't remember his name, where he lives, who his relatives and friends are, where he works, or even how to do his job. His memory loss has resulted in total disorientation, and he has become a danger both to himself and to those around him. In short, he doesn't have a clue *who he is*. Only the recovery of his memory can provide him with a sense of identity and purpose once more.

As a teacher of church history, I regularly remind my students that church history is the memory of the church and that we can't hope to understand our identity as church unless we have a well-developed Christian memory. The same principle applies in a more general way to all Christ-followers: our spiritual memory is crucial for understanding our true identity and for taking our rightful place in the true story of the whole world. For Peter, it is crucial that we should deliberately remember the truth about ourselves, perhaps particularly the truths so clearly explained in 2 Peter 1:1-4. Even though his readers are "firmly established in the truth you now have" (1:12), this is not enough for Peter in light of the threats they will face. He is passionate about exposing the dangers of spiritual amnesia. Conscious of the fact that his death is imminent, the most important item on his pastoral agenda is to "remind you of these things," "to refresh your memory," "to see that after my departure you will always be able to remember these things" (1:12, 13, 15). He will repeat the same theme again later: he asserts that he has written both of his letters as "reminders to stimulate you to wholesome thinking" (3:1).[39]

It is probably no coincidence that the Greek word *stērizō* (translated here in 2 Pet 1:12 as "firmly established") is the same word Jesus used when addressing Peter in Luke 22:32, "And when you have turned back, *strengthen* your brothers."[40] Penning the letter we know as 2 Peter was part of Peter's continuing obedience to that command. He understood that we are vulnerable when we lose our spiritual memory: to borrow Paul's words, people with spiritual amnesia are subject to being "tossed back and forth by the waves, and blown here and there by every wind of teaching and by the cunning and craftiness of people in their deceitful scheming" (Eph 4:14). The final words of this verse describe the false teachers in 2 Peter 2 exactly.

Cultivating a healthy spiritual memory is the best defense against being led astray by such false teachers and being disheartened by scoffers: "2 Peter confirms that remembering the teaching first given was a central concern in early Christianity."[41] What teaching? As Peter will show in the following verses (2 Pet 1:16–21), the words of the apostles and the prophets (broad references to the testimony of the New and Old Testaments respectively) should be at the heart of our remembering. There are regular commands in the New Testament to "remember" (for example, 1 Cor 11:2; Eph 2:11–12; 2 Tim 2:8, 14), none more pertinent than the occasion provided by the Lord's Supper to "do this in remembrance" of Jesus Christ (Luke 22:19; 1 Cor 11:23–26). Peter now adds his own voice to the call to remember.

One of the best ways of obeying the command to remember the message of Peter, and of the other apostles and prophets, is to *memorize* it. The information age has been a mixed blessing in this regard—it has prompted us to confuse access to information with actually knowing it, and so the spiritual discipline of Scripture memorization has fallen on hard times. We all know, however, that prescribed medication does us no good if we simply look at it sitting on the medicine-cabinet shelf—only when we take it into our system can it begin to do us any good. The psalmist declared, "I have hidden your word in my heart that I might not sin against you" (Ps 119:11). The word is only transformative when we take it into ourselves and it becomes part of us.[42] If you lack confidence in committing the word of Scripture to memory, remember the words of Jesus: "But the Advocate, the Holy Spirit, whom the Father will send in my name, will teach you all things and will remind you of everything I have said to you" (John 14:26).

> Cultivating a healthy spiritual memory is the best defense against being led astray by false teachers and being disheartened by scoffers.

It would be easy to overlook 2 Peter 1:12–15. At first glance, Peter's anticipation of his impending death and his desire to stir his readers' memories does not seem particularly inspiring. But nothing could be further from the truth. In fact, these verses not only provide the occasion for Peter's letter, but also represent the letter's purpose statement.[43] Further, they add another facet to the answer to Peter's question, "What sort of people ought you to be?" (2 Pet 3:11). The fact is that "memory fades fast when the pressure is on or when new and attractive teaching comes along."[44] Hence Christ-followers ought to be people who make an intentional effort to learn and remember the foundational truths of the Christian message encapsulated in the message of the apostles and prophets, because there is no better antidote to the insidious white-anting of false teachers and scoffers.

We all doubtless know people who are gullible enough to believe every hoax and conspiracy theory that makes the rounds. One concerned friend of mine regularly posts well-intentioned but misguided warnings on Facebook to protect the unsuspecting, only to retract them later when someone has referred him to the fact-checking website Snopes.com—again, we ought not to be too hard on such people, as most of us have had the wool pulled over our eyes at some stage.

Peter understood the problem well. False teachers and scoffers were peddling their pseudo-stories to his readers and shaking their spiritual foundations. As Peter will explain, these false teachers were challenging both the promised coming of Christ and the threat of future judgment (2 Pet 2:1–3:7). In the face of multiple truth-claims and conflicting stories, it can be hard to know what to believe. What is a hoax, and what is real? Where can we turn for certainty in a world of so many competing ideas? The answer is the same for us as it was for Peter's readers: the apostolic and prophetic word (2 Pet 1:16–21; see also 3:2, "I want you to recall the words spoken in the past by the holy prophets and the command given by our Lord and Savior Jesus Christ through your apostles"). The teachings of the apostles and prophets provide an essential anchor point in a culture of shifting foundations and "fake news."

The Certainty of the Apostolic Word

The first reason why Peter's readers (including those in the twenty-first century) may have confidence in the message preached by Peter and the other apostles (the emphatic "we" of 2 Pet 1:16) is that it is eyewitness testimony. As the most prominent and representative example of the apostles' firsthand experience of the grandeur of Jesus Christ, Peter has chosen the transfiguration (1:16–18).

Outside the Synoptic Gospels (Matt 17:1–8; Mark 9:2–8; Luke 9:28–36), this is the only time in the New Testament that the transfiguration is mentioned, but it stands as the summit of the apostles' recollection of the true identity of Jesus Christ in much the same way as the physical peak of the mountain of transfiguration stood out above the surrounding countryside. To the inner circle of apostles— Peter, James, and John—God had given his authenticating approval of Jesus Christ: "This is my Son, whom I love; with him I am well pleased" (2 Pet 1:17; compare also the words from heaven at Jesus' baptism in Matt 3:17; Luke 3:22). The language of the following verse emphatically underscores the point: "We ourselves heard this voice that came from heaven when we were with him on the sacred mountain" (2 Pet 1:18). When eyewitness testimony is placed in juxtaposition with the cleverly concocted fables of the false teachers, it is easy to identify the genuine product, just as counterfeit banknotes are exposed by comparison to authentic ones.

Other early church fathers employed the same argument, none more so than Irenaeus, bishop of Lyons in the late second century. Concerned for the doctrinal integrity of his and other churches in the face of rampant false teaching, he urged the readers of his *Against Heresies* (about AD 185) not to believe newfangled teachings allegedly based on secret knowledge taught by Jesus to select hearers. Rather, the teaching of Jesus to the apostles had been public from the beginning and consistently taught everywhere:

> With such clear proofs, don't go looking for the truth in other places when you can find it so easily in the church! The church is like a bank—the apostles, like wealthy people, made a huge truth-deposit into it, so that anybody regardless can make withdrawals—rivers of life. The church is the doorway to life; all others are thieves and robbers. This is why it's so important to avoid those who teach error. Rather, we must do our best to get a firm grip on the truth handed down to us. What do you reckon? Suppose there is a difference of opinion among us about some important issue. Shouldn't we refer to the oldest churches, where the apostles had the greatest input, and get their judgment on the issue? If the apostles had left us no written documents, wouldn't it make sense to comply with the teaching they themselves handed down to their successors as leaders in the churches?[45]

So don't settle for cheap imitations! Christians can have confidence in *this* word, the apostolic word, because it is the proclamation of eyewitnesses to Christ and his glory.

> Christians can have confidence in the apostolic word because it is the proclamation of eyewitnesses to Christ and his glory.

The Certainty of the Prophetic Word

If the *apostolic word* is one vital component of the firm foundation on which Christ-followers build, the *prophetic word* is the other (2 Pet 1:19–21). Sometimes in the New Testament the term "prophet" refers to a member of the church gifted by the Holy Spirit to declare God's word to the church body (1 Cor 12:28–29; Eph 3:5, 4:11; Rev 18:20). But here, the specific reference to "prophecy of Scripture" (2 Pet 1:20) and Peter's later reiteration, "I want you to recall the words spoken in the past by the holy prophets" (3:2), suggest that he has in mind the prophets of the Old Testament (and by extension, the whole Old Testament itself).[46]

Even though 2 Peter is one of the most neglected books of the New Testament, many Bible students rightly refer to 2 Peter 1:20–21 in support of the doctrine of the divine inspiration of Scripture: "Above all, you must understand that no prophecy of Scripture came about by the prophet's own interpretation of things. For prophecy never had its origin in the human will, but prophets, though human, spoke from God as they were carried along by the Holy

Spirit." That's true. But in this context Peter is arguing that the word of the prophets can be trusted to reveal the true story of the whole world authentically because these words are not just the imaginative inventions of the prophets themselves. The Holy Spirit himself enabled the words of the prophets. This makes the prophetic word, just like the apostolic word, eminently trustworthy; it too is a sure defense against false teaching: "We also have the prophetic message as something completely reliable, and you will do well to pay attention to it, as to a light shining in a dark place, until the day dawns and the morning star rises in your hearts" (2 Pet 1:19). The imagery is vivid: the prophetic word is a source of light for Peter's readers in the murkiness created by the false teachers and scoffers who have cast doubt into their minds about the coming of Jesus Christ and about future judgment. As the psalmist declares, "Your word is a lamp for my feet, a light on my path" (Ps 119:105). Peter's readers should not fear the present darkness—regardless of what the false teachers are saying, they can be certain about the future dawning of the day of the Lord (2 Pet 3:10, 12). The prophetic word shines in the darkness like Venus, the morning star, providing believers with the assurance that the day is near.

> The prophetic word is a source of light for Peter's readers in the murkiness created by the false teachers and scoffers.

To sum up, right belief matters. The proclamation of the apostles (eyewitnesses of the coming and glory of

Jesus Christ) and the prophets (carried along by the Holy Spirit) provides the substance of right belief. The purveyors of false teaching will tempt believers to abandon the true story of the whole world in favor of their own persuasive but ultimately destructive stories (2 Pet 2:1). For this reason, believers should make every effort to keep the apostolic and prophetic word fresh in their memories and alive in their behavior.

SUGGESTED READING

☐ 2 Peter 1:12–21

☐ Nehemiah 4

☐ Ephesians 6:10–20

Reflection

Peter makes a great deal of the importance of Christian memory in 2 Peter 1:13–15. Yet some Christians justify their disregard for the cultivation of a Christian memory by appealing to Paul in Philippians 3:13b–14a, "Forgetting what is behind and straining toward what is ahead, I press on toward the goal." What would be an appropriate response to such people?

_____

_____

_____

_____

Paul, like Peter, stresses that the church is "built on the foundation of the *apostles and prophets*, with Christ Jesus himself as the chief cornerstone" (Eph 2:20). What are the practical implications of this reality for believers today?

_____

_____

_____

_____

Why do you think the transfiguration is so important to Peter in arguing for the certainty of the apostles' word?

_____

_____

_____

_____

5

LOOKING OUT FOR FALSE TEACHERS

2 PETER 2:1–22

On a first reading, 2 Peter 2 appears bleak and less than inspiring, to put it mildly. It describes in blunt language the unscrupulous morals and motives of false teachers who were troubling Peter's readers, comparing them to a dog that returns to its vomit and a washed sow that goes back to wallowing in the mud (2 Pet 2:22). This is hardly the stuff of uplifting Bible studies or encouraging devotional messages. Yet an important implication of the doctrine of the inspiration of Scripture is that everything in the Bible is there because it is *meant* to be there. Peter wants his readers to have their eyes wide open about the dangers they face and to be able to recognize these dangers when they arise.

The law of Australia and many other nations emphasizes "duty of care." Persons are under an obligation to take all reasonable steps to prevent harm from coming to others. When I was driving home one rainy night, a local resident was standing in the middle of the road, directing traffic into a side-street detour because the road ahead was flooded. He was exercising his duty of care by making sure no one drove unwittingly into the floodwaters.

There are, of course, biblical precedents for exercising a duty of care. For example, if you own a dangerous bull and fail to keep it securely penned up so that it gores someone, or if you dig a pit and neglect to put a cover over it so that someone's animal falls into it, you are culpable (Exod 21:28–36). Think of Peter as exercising his apostolic duty of care to his readers in 2 Peter 2 (and, indeed, in the entire letter), warning them of the dangers they will face and making every effort to ensure their spiritual safety. The substance of 2 Peter 2 may not be pleasant, but it is necessary in order to avoid spiritual catastrophe. The Boy Scout motto "Be prepared!" applies equally to the Christian life.

> Think of Peter as exercising his apostolic duty of care to his readers in 2 Peter 2.

The chapter and verse divisions in our contemporary Bibles were not part of the original text.[47] Sometimes they obscure important connections in an author's argument. Here, Peter contrasts the certainty of the apostolic and prophetic word (2 Pet 1:16–21) with the destructiveness of the viewpoints being advanced by false teachers and scoffers (2:1–3:7). Peter wants to be certain that his readers are standing on the firm foundation laid by God as declared through the apostles and prophets. But he also wants to warn them about the seductions of false teachers who would seek to entice them away from that foundation and scoffers who would try to undermine their confidence in what they had been taught.

Dekalog (English title *The Decalogue*, 1989) is a powerful and thought-provoking ten-part television drama series commissioned by Polish television and directed by Krzysztof Kieslowski.[48] Based loosely on the Ten Commandments, each episode intriguingly explores important issues of morality and belief. In "Dekalog 1" ("You shall have no other gods before me") Warsaw shivers as Christmas approaches. Young Pawel (perhaps ten or twelve) and his father Krzysztof, an atheistic university professor, are intrigued by the power of their computer to lock and unlock doors in their apartment, turn water on and off, and answer all kinds of questions (for instance, they ask for the correct local time in a foreign location). But Pawel has bigger questions that the computer cannot answer. The death-by-freezing of a familiar neighborhood stray dog prompts Pawel (with the sympathetic ear and guidance of his aunt Irena, a devout Catholic) to ponder the meaning of life. Meantime, the local river has frozen over, and Pawel pesters his father to give him his Christmas gift early—a brand-new pair of ice skates. But is the ice thick enough for skating? Together they enter the necessary data from the weather office into their computer, which calculates that the ice is more than thick enough to support skaters. To be certain, Krzysztof himself goes out on the ice to test its strength by jumping and sliding on it. Back home, he gives a delighted Pawel the new skates. The next day, Pawel doesn't come home on time. An initially unconcerned but increasingly frantic Krzysztof tries to find Pawel, only to discover that the ice on the river has broken. He watches in despair as a rescue team pulls Pawel's lifeless body out of the water through the hole in the ice. (The screenplay, although not the movie itself, suggests that the local power station had released heated water into the river during the night.)[49] Faith in the computer and even in empirical testing did not prevent the tragedy of Pawel's drowning.

The point is that what you choose to trust *is* important; what you don't know *can* hurt you. So Peter's duty of care to his readers comprises not only a clear reminder of where their trust belongs—the truth about Jesus Christ as announced by the apostles and prophets—but also a clear warning against the error being propounded by the false teachers, and the consequences of being seduced by such error. "What sort of people ought you to be?" (2 Pet 3:11)—people who can recognize teaching and behavior that contradicts the message of the apostles and prophets about Jesus Christ; people who are vigilant and stand their ground against it due to its "destructive" nature and results (2:1). Jude makes a parallel plea: "Contend for the faith that was once for all entrusted to God's holy people" (Jude 3).[50] Taking a stand against false teaching is not popular in our tolerant age, where anything goes—but we might consider that one definition for a tolerant person is someone who has no convictions. If Peter is trying to accomplish anything in his second letter, it is to bolster his readers' conviction of the truth and to reinforce their confidence in the foundation on which they stand. Peter's impending death (2 Pet 1:13–15) adds a note of extreme urgency to this task.

The False Teachers of 2 Peter

Understandably, New Testament scholars are interested in establishing who the false teachers in 2 Peter were, because this knowledge would help us to place Peter's second letter more precisely in its historical and geographical setting. If we could identify a specific group of opponents whose characteristics match those described in 2 Peter and establish when and where such a group was active, it would help us to determine when, why, and to whom 2 Peter was written. Yet despite several proposals and plenty of detective work, the answer to this question remains elusive.[51]

From a purely practical point of view, a more productive approach is to catalog the elements of the false teaching that concern Peter and to recognize the timeless dangers and threats they pose to the people of God in *any* age or situation. (In fact, the description of the false teachers in 2 Peter 2 bears a striking resemblance to many of the false teachers of our own age.) It's helpful to think of 2 Peter as the apostolic response to the "objections" or "accusations"[52] raised by the false teachers and scoffers. They

1. reject apostolic authority;
2. fail to recognize a sinful lifestyle for what it is;
3. blasphemously discount coming judgment; and
4. deny the Lord's return.[53]

Such lists should alert Christians of every age to be on the lookout for similar teaching and to identify, expose, and guard against it. According to Peter, such vigilance is an essential quality of the transformed life. Now we can understand even better why Peter found it necessary to establish the credentials of the true prophets and apostles (including his own credentials) in 2 Peter 1:16–21, before condemning those of the false teachers. The contrast could hardly be more stark: while the gospel message proclaimed by eyewitness apostles and Holy Spirit–inspired prophets opens the way for believers to share in the life of God (2 Pet 1:4), the views peddled by the false teachers result in destruction (2:1).

> The description of the false teachers in 2 Peter 2 bears a striking resemblance to many of the false teachers of our own age.

Caveat Emptor!

In commercial transactions where property changes hands, the Latin phrase *caveat emptor*, "let the buyer beware," is often used. It means that the *buyer* is responsible for checking that the goods meet expectations. For example, you probably wouldn't dream of buying a secondhand car without taking it for a test drive and getting a mechanic to check it over. You're not going to take the salesperson's word for it. That's just common sense.

Peter wants his readers to use the same kind of common sense in spiritual matters, because the faith version of "Honest John's Used Cars" lurks everywhere.

The stakes are much higher in matters of faith, yet people often use less discernment here than in buying a used car. More than anywhere else, we need to have our eyes open and to exercise discernment in choosing what to believe.

Just as there were false prophets who tried to deceive the people of God in the Old Testament, so false teachers will confront Peter's Christ-following readers (2 Pet 2:1–3). He insists that the opinions of the false teachers are not simply neutral choices from the religious smorgasbord (a notion that appeals to many of our contemporaries). Rather, these opinions are harmful and destructive, both to the false teachers themselves and to those who gullibly follow them. Far from being "a light shining in a dark place" (1:19), as the Holy Spirit–inspired Old Testament prophets were, these false teachers obscure the truth, sow destruction, and draw the unsuspecting away from the faith with them: "Many will follow their depraved conduct" (2:2; see also 2:14, "They seduce the unstable"). In contrast to the apostles, who explicitly did *not* follow "cleverly devised stories" (1:16) because they were eyewitnesses of Jesus Christ and his glory, these false teachers "will exploit you with fabricated stories" (2:3), thus maligning the truth, confusing their hearers, and "even denying the sovereign Lord who bought them" (2:1).[54] Of course, Peter himself had at one time denied his Lord (Matt 26:69–75), so he understood from personal experience how destructive such a denial could be.

If the opinions of these pseudo-teachers were not bad enough, they add greed and exploitation to the mix (2 Pet 2:3), showing that their motives and morals are as suspect as their teaching. And although such teachers may deny it, God's judgment will certainly fall on them. Don't hesitate to put such teachings to the test, Peter seems to be saying. All that glitters is not gold. It is not a Christian virtue to be gullible or credulous. The Bereans were commended because "they examined the Scriptures every day to see if what Paul said was true" (Acts 17:11). The need for discernment based on Scripture is all the more crucial in the internet age, with its exponential proliferation of diverse viewpoints, all clamoring for a hearing.

> It is not a Christian virtue to be gullible or credulous.

Deliverance for the Righteous, but Judgment for the Ungodly

The false teachers in 2 Peter lived as though they would never be called to account for their beliefs, motives, and actions, and they were probably also actively denying the possibility of future judgment. "Where is this 'coming' he promised?" they scoffed. "Ever since our ancestors died, everything goes on as it has since the beginning of creation" (2 Pet 3:4). Against such skepticism, Peter offers a string of examples from the Old Testament (2:4–10a) to demonstrate the certainty of judgment.

Second Peter 2:4–10a is one long "if-then" sentence, with multiple "if" examples drawn from the Old Testament to back up the double-barreled "then" conclusion in 2:9: "then the Lord knows how to rescue the godly from trials and to hold the unrighteous for punishment on the day of judgment."

"If" Example	Negative: Judgment on the Unrighteous	Positive: Deliverance for the Righteous
1.	*if* God did not spare angels when they sinned (2:4)	[None]
2.	*if* God did not spare the ancient world but brought the flood on the unrighteous (2:5a)	*if* God delivered Noah, the preacher of righteousness, and seven others from the flood (2:5b)
3.	*if* God condemned the cities of Sodom and Gomorrah for their lawless deeds (2:6)	*if* God delivered righteous Lot who was distressed by the unrighteous behavior of his fellows (2:7–8)
"Then" Conclusion	*then* God knows how to hold the unrighteous for punishment of the day of judgment (2:9b)	*then* God knows how to rescue the godly from trials (2:9a)

One of the enduring values of the Old Testament for Christian believers is that it provides a rich array of examples to follow or avoid, as the case may be. Writing of the failures of the Israelites during their wilderness wanderings, Paul makes the point this way: "These things happened to them as examples and were written down as warnings for us" (1 Cor 10:11; see also v. 6). Peter wants his readers to understand that there is a clear historical pattern in the Old Testament of judgment for the ungodly and deliverance for the righteous. The false teachers intended to deny the reality of judgment by arguing that "ever since our ancestors died, everything goes on as it has since the beginning of creation" (2 Pet 3:4), but Peter's catalog of Old Testament examples makes it clear that they were ignoring history in making such a claim. Once again, the reliability of the prophetic word is affirmed (see 1:19–21), as is Peter's Old Testament conceptual framework.[55]

> "The Lord knows how to rescue the godly from trials and to hold the unrighteous for punishment on the day of judgment."
>
> —2 Peter 2:9

Recognizing False Teachers by Their Fruit

"Every good tree bears good fruit," declared Jesus, "but a bad tree bears bad fruit. A good tree cannot bear bad fruit, and a bad tree cannot bear good fruit. ... Thus, by their fruit you will know them" (Matt 7:17–18, 20; see also Luke 6:43–45). The fruit of the false teachers in

2 Peter 2:10b–22 is plain to see, and it should be obvious what kind of people they are: bold and arrogant (v. 10b), disrespectful and blasphemous (vv. 11–12), sensual and driven by natural instinct (vv. 12, 14), brazen in their pursuit of pleasure (v. 13), greedy and deluded by the temporary payout of wickedness, as Balaam was (vv. 14–16; see Num 22:4–24:25). They promise much but deliver little (2 Pet 2:17–19)—like candy floss or cotton candy, they offer a momentary rush of sweetness, followed by emptiness.

What is even worse, they entice others to follow them in this wanton lifestyle. It is especially tragic when people "who are just escaping from those who live in error" (2:18) are drawn back into the very same error. As every drug addict or alcoholic knows only too well, the "freedom" to use such substances is only a thin disguise for bondage; "people are slaves to whatever has mastered them" (2:19). How crucial it is to choose the right master! I recall my father's grief when, as a pastor, he had helped an unchurched family come to faith in Christ, only for them to be hijacked almost immediately by a sect. Peter suggests that it would be better for such people not to have known the way of righteousness at all than, having come to know it, be drawn back into destructive error once again (2:20–21). It is such apostasy that prompts Peter's use of the somewhat disgusting and thus striking metaphors of a dog returning to its vomit and a washed sow returning to wallow in the mud (2:22).

How do passages such as 2 Peter 2 help us to live transformed lives and enable us to find a God-glorifying answer to Peter's question, "What kind of people ought you to be?" (2 Pet 3:11). First, this chapter provides a fairly dramatic portrait of the kind of person a Christ-follower should *not* be. If ever there were an example of the kind of behavior Christians should avoid, surely this is it. There is an explicit warning here not to live this way, nor to be taken in by those who do, regardless of how attractive they may make it sound. In Paul's words, "So, if you think you are standing firm, be careful that you don't fall!" (1 Cor 10:12). If ever we are tempted to ask, "Shall we sin because we are not under the law but under grace?" (Rom 6:15), 2 Peter 2 teaches us to respond with just as much fervor as Paul, "By no means!" (The entire paragraph of Romans 6:15–23 is good commentary on 2 Peter 2.) The antidote to false teaching and false living is to be solidly grounded in the apostolic and prophetic word (2 Pet 1:16–21). Yes, even the bleak and forbidding apostolic word of 2 Peter 2.

> The antidote to false teaching and false living is to be solidly grounded in the apostolic and prophetic word.

Second, it would be a mistake, in my opinion, to drag passages such as 2 Peter 2:20–22 into the "once saved, always saved" versus "you can lose your salvation" debate. Peter has already described the God-given foundation that is the basis of our Christian assurance (see especially 1:1–4), but he also finds it necessary to sound a clear warning about the dangers of apostasy (as the writer of Hebrews does in the warning passages in Heb 2:1–4; 3:7–4:13; 5:11–6:12; 10:19–39; 12:14–29). We live our Christian lives in glad confidence about what God has done for us in

Christ, but we take seriously the warnings against turning back to the old life from which we have been delivered (see also 2 Pet 3:17).

Finally, the negative portrayal of the false teachers and their followers in 2 Peter 2 provides the backdrop against which the "godly life" (1:3) stands out in stark contrast. We are not merely to be pale reflections of the world out of which we have been called. On the contrary! As Peter puts it in his first letter, "But you are a chosen people, a royal priesthood, a holy nation, God's special possession, that you may declare the praises of him who called you out of darkness into his wonderful light" (1 Pet 2:9). What kind of people ought you to be? A countercultural people who are distinct from the world, but who exist for the sake of the world.

SUGGESTED READING

- ☐ 2 Peter 2:1–22
- ☐ Proverbs 14:12
- ☐ Matthew 7:15–20
- ☐ Jude

Reflection

Someone says to you, "I don't understand why Peter spends so much time talking about false teachers. It seems so negative. Surely, if we are grounded in the truth, that's all we need!" Based on your reading of 2 Peter 2, how would you respond?

_____

_____

_____

At the heart of 2 Peter 2 are the twin truths that "the Lord knows how to rescue godly people from trials and to hold the unrighteous for the day of judgment" (2:9). Yet many people have problems with Christianity at precisely these points: godly people often face huge difficulties, sometimes in the long term, and evil people often seem to prosper. How does Peter answer these concerns?

_____

_____

_____

What, according to Peter, are the fruits of false teachers? Where can you see such fruits being borne today?

_____

_____

_____

6

RESISTING SCOFFERS

2 PETER 3:1–10

It's almost impossible to miss Peter's increasing urgency and passion for his message as his second letter draws toward its conclusion. His tone has become progressively more personal as he has moved from a fairly general form of address at the beginning, to those "who have received a faith as precious as ours" (1:1), to "brothers and sisters" (1:10), and now to "dear friends" in chapter 3. The word translated "dear friends" (*agapētoi* in the Greek) literally means "beloved" and reflects the closeness of relationships within the body of Christ (recall "love" in 2 Pet 1:7 as the crowning Christian character virtue). The word appears five times in this chapter, in verses 1, 8, 14, 15 (of Paul), and 17. Strikingly, it is the same word used of Jesus Christ by God's voice from heaven at the transfiguration (literally, "this is my beloved Son"; 2 Pet 1:17). Sharing in the same belovedness that the Father expresses for his Son is one of the great privileges of being Christ-followers and perhaps shines more light on what it means to "participate in the divine nature" (2 Pet 1:4). Be that as it may, Peter continues in this chapter to express his duty of care toward his ancient and contemporary readers by bolstering their resistance to those who mock and question their Christian faith.

Repeating Important Themes

As you read 2 Peter 3:1-2 you may well think you have been here before—not just because Peter says that this is now the "second letter"[56] he is writing to his readers (2 Pet 3:1-2), but also because he revisits some themes that by now are very familiar in this letter. As every teacher knows, repetition is an essential means of getting information to stick in the minds of learners, and Peter uses repetition to good effect.

> Repetition is an essential means of getting information to stick in the minds of learners, and Peter uses repetition to good effect.

First, he underscores yet again the importance of cultivating a good Christian memory, positively by encouraging his readers to *remember* what he is writing to them, and negatively by urging them *not to forget*. Consider the prominence of these themes in 2 Peter:

Remember!	Don't forget!
"So I will always *remind* you of these things" (1:12)	Those who do not cultivate the virtues of the Christian life are *forgetting* that they have been cleansed from their past sins" (1:9)
"I think it is right to *refresh your memory*" (1:13)	Scoffers "deliberately *forget*" the judgment of the sinful world by the flood (3:5)
"I will make every effort to see that after my departure you will always be able to *remember* these things" (1:15)	"Do not *forget*" that the Lord operates according to a higher timetable than ours (3:8)
"You will do well to *pay attention* to [the prophetic message]" (1:19)	
"I have written both of [my letters] as *reminders*" (3:1)	
"I want you to *recall* the words [of the prophets and the apostles]" (3:2)	

Viewed all together in this way, the effect is powerful. The best way to stand firm in the Christian life and to grow in it, and at the same time to resist seductive false teaching and mockery of the Christian faith, is to remember and not forget.

Remember *what*? Here is the *second* piece of familiar territory: "I want you to recall the words spoken in the past by the holy *prophets* and the command given by our Lord and Savior through your *apostles*" (2 Pet 3:2). Once again Peter emphasizes the importance of the apostolic and prophetic word (2 Pet 1:16–21) as the foundation of truth on which Christ-followers stand and the armor by means of which they protect themselves from seductive false teaching and the mockery of skeptics. There simply isn't any substitute for grounding ourselves solidly in the trustworthy word of the Scriptures, or, putting it differently, living consistently in accordance with God's true story, of which we are part.

For Peter, the purpose of remembering the truth as communicated by apostles and the prophets is "to stimulate you to wholesome thinking," or, more literally, "stirring up your *sincere minds* by way of reminder" (2 Pet 3:2). This is a word we need to hear in the experience- and action-driven Christianity of our day, where the cultivation of the Christian mind is often treated with neglect, disdain, and even suspicion. (I recall a concerned old man at our church telling me that seminary would "ruin" me.) "The scandal of the evangelical mind," laments Mark Noll (with perhaps deliberate exaggeration), "is that there is not much of an evangelical mind."[57] This is despite the teaching of Jesus, "Love the Lord your God with all your heart and with all your soul *and with all your mind*" (Matt 22:37; see also Mark 12:30; Luke 10:27), and Paul's exhortation, "Do not be conformed any longer to the pattern of this world, but *be transformed by the renewing of your mind*" (Rom 12:2). Harry Blamires reminds us that "the Christian mind is the prerequisite of Christian thinking. And Christian thinking is the prerequisite of Christian action."[58] Peter would agree. It is crucially important for Christ-followers to cultivate "wholesome thinking" (2 Pet 3:1), and the raw material for such thinking is the prophetic and apostolic word. What kind of people ought we to be (2 Pet 3:11)? People who hear and obey the call to cultivating good, healthy Christian thinking.

That's not to say, of course, that authentic Christianity is *only* about the mind. Christianity is also very much about the heart and its desires. Whenever in Christian history there has been an overemphasis on the intellectual or brain-based dimension of Christian faith (like the scholasticism of the High Middle Ages or the arid Protestant rationalism of the seventeenth century), there has been an inevitable spiritual or heart reaction (such as medieval Christian mysticism or Protestant Pietism). Peter is not suggesting that it's enough to know the prophetic and the apostolic word—faithful Christ-following requires trust and a response of faithful living. But here he is addressing issues of false *teaching* and thus is stressing the importance of orthodox and wholesome *thinking*.

Forewarned Is Forearmed!

By way of contrast, it is distinctly *un*wholesome thinking to allege, as the scoffers do (2 Pet 3:3-4), that the second coming of Jesus (and hence the judgment too) is bogus. To make things worse, they also follow "their own evil desires" (3:3)—if there is no judgment, why not live as you please? The combination of mockery on the one hand and a seductively licentious lifestyle on the other comprises a potentially lethal attack on Christ-followers.

In the "last days" (an expression that refers to the entire period between the first and second comings of the Lord Jesus Christ) such attacks will be inevitable, which is why Peter wants his readers to be particularly alert: "*Above all*, you must understand that in the last days scoffers will come" (2 Pet 3:3). But forewarned is fore-armed—early warning gives people the opportunity to prepare defenses against approaching danger. The importance of not being caught offguard is a repeated theme in the General Epistles: "Do not be surprised at the fiery ordeal that has come on you" (1 Pet 4:12); "Do not be surprised, my brothers and sisters, if the world hates you" (1 John 3:13). And Peter will underscore the same point at the end of his second letter: "Since you have been fore-warned, be on your guard" (2 Pet 3:17).

> Forewarned is forearmed—early warning gives people the opportunity to prepare defenses against approaching danger.

So, *expect* to hear scoffers say that since the second coming and the judgment haven't happened, they *won't* happen: "Where is this 'coming' he promised? Ever since our ancestors died, everything goes on as it has since the beginning of creation" (2 Pet 3:4). But, as Peter explains, such a viewpoint represents both a poor grasp of history (3:5-7) and poor thinking about God's program and timetable (3:8-10).

The Scoffers' Poor Grasp of History

The first line of defense against the scoffers is understanding that they are in error when they suggest that "everything goes on as it has since the beginning of creation" (2 Pet 3:4). Not so! They forget the judgment that took place at the time of Noah's flood (2 Pet 3:5-6; see Gen 6-8; 2 Pet 2:5), and they also forget the judgment meted out on the evil angels and the evil cities of Sodom and Gomorrah (2 Pet 2:4, 6-9). Many other examples of God's righteous judgment on evil could be cited from the Old Testament. It's not that the scoffers are just having an excusable lapse of memory; they "deliberately forget" (3:5) these historical instances of judgment that came about by God's dictate. Or, as Peter Davids translates it, "they consciously avoid noticing this."[59] In short, they are intentionally living their lives according to the wrong story. Since the historical examples of God's judgment on the ungodly do not suit their agenda, they willfully suppress the evidence. This in itself is sufficient to expose them as charlatans, as purveyors of "fabricated stories" (2:3). But there's more.

The Scoffers' Poor Thinking about God's Program and Timetable

The faulty logic of the scoffers is that if something has never happened before, it *won't* happen. To them, the delay in the second coming of Christ proves that the promise of his return is null and void. How long can you live in hope without giving up hope and inventing a new story for yourself?

It's all too easy to succumb to arguments like this. So, as we might well expect from Peter by now, he urges his readers not to forget a vital component of the true story by which they should live: "But do not forget this one thing, dear friends: With the Lord a day is like a thousand years, and a thousand years are like a day" (2 Pet 3:8; see also Ps 90:4). The Lord works according to a different timetable from ours. (In fact, time is part of the created order, and God stands above and beyond it in eternity, so that every point on the time continuum is "present" to him.) If they only knew that the delay is a sign not of the failure of the promise but of God's patience in allowing more time for more people to repent (2 Pet 3:9; see also v. 15a; 1 Tim 2:4; Rom 2:4). If God is "slow" at anything, he is slow to anger (Exod 34:6–7). Some may persist in their evil ways and perish, but that is not God's desire.[60] Nor should it be ours.

The Day of the Lord

If Peter's readers have been paying attention to the words of the prophets and the apostles, as he has been urging them to do (2 Pet 1:16–21; 3:2), the idea of "the day of the Lord" (2 Pet 3:10) should be familiar to them (for example, Jer 46:10; Amos 5:18–20; Zeph 1:14–16; 1 Cor 3:13; 1 Thess 5:2; 2 Thess 2:2). The day of the Lord could denote a day of judgment on Israel or one of the surrounding nations, but all of the lesser days reach their culmination in the final day of the Lord when Jesus Christ returns.

> Even though the return of Christ and the judgment
> are delayed from a human viewpoint, the day of the
> Lord will come, and judgment with it.

The ancient world of Noah's time met its judgment in the flood (2 Pet 3:6). Similarly, the present world will meet its judgment in fire (2 Pet 3:7, 10), despite everything appearing to go on as it has since time immemorial (2 Pet 3:4). (We will have to say more about this in chapter 7.) Even though the return of Christ and the judgment are delayed from a human viewpoint—to hold open the door to repentance for as long as possible—the day of the Lord *will* come, and judgment with it. Like a thief, the day of the Lord will arrive unexpectedly (2 Pet 3:10a), so people should be ready for it all the time (see also Matt 24:43; Luke 12:39–40; 1 Thess 5:2–4). Forewarned is indeed forearmed!

SUGGESTED READING

☐ 2 Peter 3:1–10

☐ Psalm 1

☐ Amos 5:18–27

☐ 1 Thessalonians 5:1–11

Reflection

How should we balance our longing for the Lord's return (especially if we are in difficult circumstances) with the awareness that the delay in his return means further opportunity for people to repent (2 Pet 3:9)?

_____

_____

_____

_____

We have all probably been confronted with scoffers. What, according to Peter, is the best way to deal with them?

_____

_____

_____

_____

7

LIVING IN LIGHT OF THE END

2 PETER 3:11–18

Long-distance running taught me many important life lessons. One of those lessons was to orient my life—my training, nutrition, and other habits—toward the date of the marathon many months in advance. I learned to live in anticipation of the test that would arrive on race day, working backward from that date to construct a training program and to cultivate habits that would get me ready for the race in good time. I was motivated to put up with all those early mornings, steep hills, sore muscles, and blisters because I knew I would benefit from that huge investment of time and energy on race day. In other words, I was living in light of the end represented by the race itself.

Of course, all of this makes good sense in many other areas of life. In anticipation of the final examination, students (the diligent ones, anyway!) work out a study program for the entire semester; farmers know that they must plan the entire planting and growing season carefully in order to reap a good crop at the time of harvest. They are living *now* in light of the coming *end*, taking a backward view from the anticipated end to plan how to live in the present. One of Stephen Covey's celebrated habits of highly effective people is, "Begin with the end in mind." He explains: "To begin with the end in mind means to start with a clear understanding of your destination. It means to know where you're going so that you better understand where you are now and so that the steps you take are always in the right direction."[61]

Ethics and Eschatology: "What Kind of People Ought You to Be?"

According to Peter, the very same principle of beginning with the end in mind also holds true in the Christian life. The end is the promised return of the Lord Jesus Christ and the judgment. In light of the coming end, Peter asks the searching question, "What kind of people ought you to be?" (2 Pet 3:11). As we have seen, Peter's entire letter is aimed at answering this question (see the suggested outline of 2 Peter at the end of the introduction). But the question comes into particularly sharp focus when we consider it in light of the *end* of the true story of the whole world. As Green points out, "Our author does not engage in speculation about the timing of forthcoming eschatological events. He rather sees the final events of the world ... as motivation for Christian conduct. As in other passages of the [New Testament], *Christian ethics are rooted within eschatology.*"[62]

> "[Peter] does not engage in speculation about the timing of forthcoming eschatological events. He rather sees the final events of the world … as motivation for Christian conduct."
>
> —Michael Green

The problem with the false teachers and the scoffers is that they deny the ending of the true story, God's story, and without a right understanding of that end they do not and cannot live as they should. The contrast between the two ways to live, as Peter has consistently described them throughout his letter, could hardly be more vivid. Will we conduct our lives in accordance with God's true story as revealed in the words of the apostles and prophets, or will we follow the cleverly devised stories and destructive opinions of the false prophets and scoffers?

Ruth Anne Reese rightly reminds us:

> The voice of 2 Peter is an ethical voice. It calls us to live out knowing Jesus, and it asks us to do this despite a generally hostile world. More than that it calls us to live out the way of Jesus when the world is shouting at us that life is better apart from the knowledge of Jesus. The arguments and topics addressed in 2 Peter all come back to the same issue, "What sort of people ought we to be?" (3:11).[63]

Peter spells out his ethical vision for the transformed life repeatedly in his letter: leading a "godly life" as we participate in the divine nature (2 Pet 1:3–4); cultivating

Christian virtues (1:5–7); avoiding the negative example set by the false teachers and scoffers (2:1–3:7); living a life that is "spotless, blameless and at peace with him" (3:14). The false teachers advocate something quite different. They are "blots and blemishes" (2:13), they deliberately ignore God's true story of the whole world (no second coming, no judgment), and they conduct themselves as people who are clearly not at peace with God. Being a Christ-follower demands a complete rejection of their false story.

When exactly the "day of God" (2 Pet 3:12) will come is known to God alone. The false teachers were using the delay in its coming as evidence that the very idea of the second coming of Christ and the judgment should be rejected, but Peter has already made it clear that this apparent delay (from the human perspective) is a reflection of God's patience in allowing more time for people to repent (2 Pet 3:4, 9). Now he provides the counterpoint by teaching that believers can "speed its coming" (3:12). The apparent tension is resolved if we understand that "the repentant behavior of Christians, characterized by lives of 'holiness and godliness,' 'hastens' the 'coming day of God.' Simply put, as more repent, the day draws closer."[64] "What kind of people ought you to be?" (3:11). On the one hand, we are grateful that in God's timetable he has held the door to repentance open for so long—to include even people such as us! On the other hand, we long for his appearing (2 Tim 4:8) and speed its coming by living holy and godly lives that display the fruit of repentance.

"A New Heaven and a New Earth"

Together with Isaiah (65:17; 66:22) and John in Revelation (21:1), Peter teaches that Christian believers look forward to "a new heaven and a new earth, where righteousness dwells" (2 Pet 3:13). But what exactly does this mean, and how does the transition from this obviously corrupted and decaying universe to a new heaven and a new earth happen? Many interpreters of Scripture have taught that the language of 2 Peter 3 points toward the complete annihilation of the present physical universe: "the present heavens and earth are reserved for fire" (3:7); "the heavens will disappear [or pass away] with a roar; the elements will be destroyed by fire" (3:10); "everything will be destroyed in this way" (3:11); "that day will bring about the destruction of the heavens by fire, and the elements will melt in the heat" (3:12).

> Second Peter 3 teaches not the annihilation of the created universe but its transformation.

But such a viewpoint is not as self-evident as it might seem. In a helpful article, Matthew Emerson summarizes the viewpoint, held by many Christian teachers down through the centuries, that 2 Peter 3 teaches not the annihilation of the created universe but its transformation.[65] Just as the flood did not annihilate the earth but judged and purified it, so the final fire of judgment will destroy evil from the earth (3:5–7), bringing forth a new heaven and a new earth where righteousness dwells (3:13). N. T. Wright explains,

> Peter is not saying that the present world of space, time and matter is going to be burnt up and destroyed. ... What will happen, as many early Christian teachers said, is that some sort of "fire," literal or metaphorical, will come upon the whole earth, not to destroy, but to test everything out, and to purify it by burning up everything that doesn't meet the test.[66]

It is not clear what precisely the elements are that will be destroyed. Wright suggests that they are the parts of creation that are needed for heat and light (sun, moon, and stars; see Isa 34:4); in the new creation they won't be needed (see Rev 21:23-24).[67] What is clear is that judgment is inevitable and that people should be prepared for it. Recall the function of the fire of judgment in 1 Corinthians 3:12-15—it destroys worthless works (represented by wood, hay, and straw) but authenticates what has been built with quality and care (gold, silver, and precious stones). So here, "the earth and everything in it will be laid bare" or exposed to the fires of judgment and seen for what it really is (2 Pet 3:10). The clear implication is to mind what we build on the foundation. We should not be investing ourselves in what the fire of judgment will consume.

Yet despite the evil and corruption that has befallen the created order due to human sinfulness, God continues to love and care for it, and the ultimate future of Christ-followers lies not in a disembodied state in heaven (at best a temporary abode for the righteous dead in the presence of God) but in a restored and transformed earth in which God makes his dwelling among the redeemed (Rev 21:1–5). The notion of escape from an evil, material world into the good, spiritual realm where God lives owes more to ancient Greek philosophy and aberrations such as Gnosticism than it does to the message of the apostles and prophets. The thoroughly unbiblical disdain for creation that has dogged too much Christian thought has resulted in the wanton exploitation of the world, rather than a caring stewardship of it. If it's all going to be destroyed anyway, many people think, why look after it? Such a notion runs counter to Peter's vision of a restored creation or, as Paul has it, the hope "that the creation itself will be liberated from its bondage to decay and be brought into the freedom and glory of the children of God" (Rom 8:21).

A Parting Exhortation

The words "so then" (2 Pet 3:14) and "therefore" (3:17) alert Peter's readers that his final exhortations will be squarely based on everything that has gone before. In particular, these verses provide summary answers to the question, "What kind of people ought you to be?" (3:11).

First, in confident anticipation of the new heavens and the new earth, believers should "make every effort" (a favorite expression of Peter; see also 1:5, 10, 15) to live lives that are "spotless, blameless, and at peace with him" (2 Pet 3:14), in marked contrast to the false teachers, who are "blots and blemishes" (2:13). The future hope of believers always calls for holy living in the present. If we are discouraged because of the delay in Christ's return, we are to remember that "our Lord's patience means salvation" (3:15; recall v. 9). We don't want to see evil people getting what we think they deserve, since we too were deserving of judgment. The delay in the day of judgment has given us time to repent, just as we trust they too will be given time. The patience of God in desiring repentance is a common theme in both Peter and Paul as bearers of the common apostolic message (see, for example, Rom 2:4; 3:25); and both Peter and Paul have experienced the distortion of their message by false teachers.[68] Some of Peter's readers will doubtless be relieved to know that for even Peter there were some things in Paul's letters that are difficult to understand (2 Pet 3:16)! At the same time, Peter regards the authority of Paul's letters as being on a par "with the other Scriptures" (that is, the Old Testament). Once again Peter affirms the integrity, authority, and essential unity of the apostolic and prophetic word (see also 1:16–21; 3:2).

> The future hope of believers always calls for holy living in the present.

Second, in light of the white-anting activities of the false teachers and scoffers, believers are told to be on their guard so that they won't be swept away by "the error of the lawless" (2 Pet 3:17; see 2:18). Second Peter is a letter of warning; believers need to beware of seductive false teaching. Peter's duty of care will not allow him to soft-pedal the dangers. It sounds like a contradiction in terms to "fall from your secure position" (3:17)—if it's secure, how can you fall from it?—but that is what can happen, Peter asserts, when you fail to take the necessary precautions against false teaching. Faced as we are in our day with a smorgasbord of religious ideas and the postmodern notion that there is no objective truth, Peter's warning needs to be taken with utmost seriousness. Forewarned is forearmed—but we need to take the warning seriously to be armed properly.

Yet despite the importance of the warning sounded in 2 Peter, the letter ends on a positive note. Just as the best protection against weeds in your lawn is flourishing, healthy grass, so too the best protection against false teaching and apostasy is healthy growth in the Christian life: "Grow in the grace and knowledge of the Lord Jesus Christ" (2 Pet 3:18). In this closing exhortation, Peter returns to some of the themes at the beginning of his letter, bookending it neatly with "grace" and "the knowledge of the Lord Jesus Christ" (compare 1:2, 8), and with the growth that is implied by the necessity of adding to our faith the Christian virtues (compare 1:5–8). It is easy enough, perhaps, to understand how to grow in knowledge of the Lord Jesus Christ.[69] An intentional and increasing familiarity with the message of the apostles and prophets about Jesus should be a priority for Christ-followers. But what about growing in grace? If grace by definition is a benefit conferred freely, how do we grow in it? In the context of 2 Peter, the answer probably has much to do with the intentional cultivation of the Christian virtues or "graces" (1:5–8).

Fittingly, Peter closes his letter with a doxology: literally, "To him [our Lord and Savior Jesus Christ] be the glory both now and into the day of eternity" (2 Pet 3:18, my translation). Not many New Testament letters end with doxologies (the exceptions are Rom 16:25–27; Phil 4:20; Jude 24–25), and these doxologies are directed to God the Father. Peter's doxology reflects his high view of Jesus Christ, another bookend reflecting his belief in Jesus as "our God and Savior" (see 1:1). And instead of the conventional "forever and ever" in such doxologies, Peter says "into the day of eternity," a final reminder of the coming day of God—the climax of the true story, and the doorway into the new heaven and the new earth. Hence, even the doxology is Peter's final effort to make us consider what kind of people we ought to be and how we ought to live in light of the coming end.

SUGGESTED READING

- ☐ 2 Peter 3:11–18
- ☐ Isaiah 65:17–25; 66:22–23
- ☐ Revelation 21
- ☐ 1 Corinthians 15:50–58

Reflection

Does it come as a surprise to you that Peter's discussion of the day of the Lord climaxes in the question, "What kind of people ought you to be?" (2 Pet 3:11)? Why, or why not?

_____

_____

_____

Peter "sees the final events of the world … as motivation for Christian conduct" (Michael Green). In his first letter, Peter reminds his readers that "the end of all things is near" (1 Pet 4:7). What response to our awareness of the approaching end does Peter urge in 2 Peter and in 1 Peter 4:7–11?

_____

_____

_____

What do you think Peter means when he tells us to "grow in the grace and knowledge of our Lord and Savior Jesus Christ" (2 Pet 3:18)? What other passages in 2 Peter suggest answers to this question?

_____

_____

_____

CONCLUSION

We can all probably relate to the experience of Christian in John Bunyan's justifiably renowned *The Pilgrim's Progress* (first published in 1678). Agonizing over an intolerable burden of sin he bears on his back, and longing to be free of it, he takes the advice of Evangelist and sets off from the City of Destruction toward the Celestial City.

But his journey is far from easy. Although there are some characters who encourage him on his way (such as Help, Good-Will, and Interpreter), there are others who gaslight him and make him seriously wonder whether he is following the right path after all (characters such as Pliable, Obstinate, and Mr. Worldly Wiseman). Here's what Mr. Worldly Wiseman says to Christian (the English comes from the 1600s, but the ideas are as fresh as today's newspaper): "Hear me, I am older than thou; thou art like to meet with, in the way which thou goest, wearisomeness, painfulness, hunger, perils, nakedness, sword, lions, dragons, darkness, and, in a word, death, and what not! These things are certainly true, having been confirmed by many testimonies. And why should a man so carelessly cast away himself, by giving heed to a stranger?" (§40). And, "But why wilt thou seek for ease this way, seeing so many dangers attend it? especially since, hadst thou but patience to hear me, I could direct thee to the obtaining of what thou desirest, without the dangers that thou in this way wilt run thyself into; yea, and the remedy is at hand. Besides, I will add, that instead of those dangers, thou shalt meet with much safety, friendship, and content" (§42).[70]

Poor Christian! Whom should he believe? Or (to put the question as we framed it in the introduction to this book), who will get to narrate the story of his life? Which story is true?

Second Peter is written for people like Christian, and us, who need to be reminded about the true story in the midst of all the false alternatives that swirl around us. Reread the whole brief letter now. Listen to Peter as he fulfills the commission given to him by Jesus in John 21:15–19, to provide good nourishment for God's flock. Commit yourself again to living in accordance with God's true story of the whole world, as mediated to us by the apostles and prophets, and brought afresh to our memories by the brief but hugely important, transformative letter of 2 Peter.

SUGGESTED READING

- ☐ 2 Peter
- ☐ 1 Corinthians 1:18–25
- ☐ Ephesians 4:1
- ☐ Colossians 1:9–10

Reflection

Recall Peter's searching question, "What kind of people ought you to be?" (2 Pet 3:11). Revisit the outline of 2 Peter in the introduction to this book and list the answers Peter gives to his question through his letter.

_____

_____

_____

_____

Join fervently with Peter in his benediction in 2 Peter 3:18: "To him [our Lord and Savior Jesus Christ] be glory both now and forever! Amen."

_____

_____

_____

_____

APPENDIX: CRITICAL ISSUES IN STUDYING 2 PETER

You don't have to dig far beneath the surface of 2 Peter before you encounter some significant problems. Even so conservative a scholar as Donald Guthrie writes:

> This is the most problematical of all the New Testament Epistles because of early doubts concerning its authenticity and because internal evidence is considered by many to substantiate those doubts. In short, the majority of scholars reject it as a genuine work of the apostle Peter, in spite of its own claims, and regard it as a later pseude-pigraphon [a document written under a false name or pseudonym].[71]

Spelling things out in a little more detail, the problems include the following:

- Many scholars (including some evangelicals) question whether the apostle Peter was—or could have been—the author of one or both of the letters that go by his name, and whether on historical and other grounds these letters could have been written within Peter's lifetime. For instance, the author already seems to be aware of a collection of Paul's letters (2 Pet 3:15–16), and (it is alleged) such a collection could not yet have existed as early as the time of Peter's martyrdom in the mid-to-late 60s under the Roman emperor Nero.

- If the apostle Peter was not the author, then someone else has used his name (2 Pet 1:1). The technical term for the practice of writing under someone else's name is "pseudepigraphy." It was quite a common practice in the ancient world. But when it comes to a canonical document such as 2 Peter, was pseudepigraphy a legitimate practice or a deliberate attempt to deceive?

- It was not uncommon in the ancient world for a follower or followers of a prominent but now-deceased person to compose a "testament" or "farewell speech" in the name of the deceased person in order to perpetuate their teaching after their death. People of the time understood what a testament was and wouldn't have regarded it as a deliberate attempt to deceive. It has been suggested that 2 Peter is such a testament.[72]

- How could Peter, an uneducated Jewish Galilean fisherman, write such sophisticated Greek and produce a document whose style reflects classical Greek rhetoric? The differing style and themes of 1 and 2 Peter are further complications.

- The originality of 2 Peter has been questioned, since a large part of it (2:1–3:4) seems to be adapted from Jude (or possibly vice versa).

- Second Peter was the last of the New Testament documents to be recognized as belonging to the canon of Scripture, suggesting that there were questions in the church of the first few centuries about its integrity and value.

- Some scholars regard 2 Peter's theological contribution as limited at best, or even questionable. Specifically, 2 Peter has been characterized as "harsh, even uncontrolled polemic offering only undisciplined rants against unorthodox Christian teachers."[73]

Because of these difficulties, most New Testament scholarship has simply adopted the viewpoint of Ernst Käsemann that 2 Peter is "perhaps the most dubious writing in the canon."[74] Peter Davids justifiably laments that 2 Peter has thus been stereotyped as the "ugly stepchild" of the New Testament.[75] This stigma attached to 2 Peter is probably the main reason why, until comparatively recently, it has received so little attention (recall the brief discussion in the introduction under the heading, "Why 2 Peter?").

What are sincere and thoughtful readers of the New Testament to make of these issues? Some well-meaning students of the Bible regard it as sacrilege to ask such searching questions of biblical documents such as 2 Peter. Others see such questioning as a not-so-subtle liberal conspiracy to undermine the authority of Scripture. "It's in the Bible," they reply. "God says it, I believe it, that settles it." But it's in no one's interest to sweep these questions under the rug or to pretend they don't exist. Obscurantism is not a Christian virtue! We honor Scripture by asking serious questions of it. We can't definitively solve every question that has been raised about 2 Peter, but this is not a good reason to retreat from them. In fact, a careful examination of the evidence can provide good reasons to conclude that the apostle Peter is, in fact, the author of the two New Testament letters that bear his name, and hence that these letters must be dated within his own lifetime (the mid-to-late 60s at the latest).

This is obviously not the place to attempt to provide a detailed response to all of the issues listed above. Those who would like to see such responses in more detail may be interested to read the online articles by Michael J. Kruger, "The Authenticity of 2 Peter," and Daniel B. Wallace, "Second Peter: Introduction, Argument, Outline."[76] But the following points can be made, even if only to prove the point that there is no definitive reason to reject the authenticity of 2 Peter and that the claims the letter makes for itself may be taken at face value:

- The author identifies himself as "Simeon Peter" (2 Pet 1:1). This less common variant of his name (Simeon, rather than Simon) appears elsewhere only once in the New Testament, in Acts 15:14.[77] Someone wanting to impersonate him (a pseudepigrapher) would almost certainly have used the much more common "Simon."

There are several personal references in the letter that hint at the apostle Peter as the author. Peter's awareness of his impending death (2 Pet 1:15-17) reflects the word of Jesus to him in John 21:18-19 (although he may well have received a more recent revelation of this, just before writing 2 Peter). He claims to be an eyewitness of the signs and wonders attached to the ministry of Jesus (2 Pet 1:16) and refers specifically to the transfiguration as an example of this (1:17-18), deliberately using the first person: "*We ourselves* heard this voice that came from heaven when *we* were with him on the sacred mountain." When the author says that "this is now my second letter to you" (3:1), the natural inference is that 1 Peter was the first (although this too is debated), and that the same person was the author of both. It's not too much of a stretch to recognize in the author's sense of urgency (apparent at many points in the letter) a heartfelt response to Jesus' words to Peter, "But I have prayed for you, Simon, that your faith may not fail. And when you have turned back, strengthen your brothers" (Luke 22:32), and the repeated "Feed my lambs. ... Take care of my sheep. ... Feed my sheep" in Jesus' reinstatement of Peter (John 21:15-17).

- Second Peter shows similarities with the "testament" or "farewell speech" genre of literature, and many such testaments are known to be pseudepigraphical. But 2 Peter is first of all a letter. According to Carson and Moo, all the evidence we possess suggests that pseudepigraphical letters were not common in the first or second centuries and that the few we know about were rejected as forgeries. ... The very fact that 2 Peter was accepted as a canonical book, then, presumes that the early Christians who made this decision were sure that Peter wrote it.[78]

- Before we jump to the conclusion that the language and style of 2 Peter make it impossible for Peter, an "uneducated" Galilean fisherman, to have written it, we should bear the following in mind. The use of Greek was not as uncommon in Galilee as is often thought; since the Greek conquest of the eastern Mediterranean region under Alexander the Great and the gradual hellenization of the area (especially under Antiochus IV Epiphanes from 198 BC onward), Greek became the language of business and commerce, and Peter would have had to know at least some Greek.[79] Furthermore, we know virtually nothing about Peter's life between the Jerusalem Council (Acts 15:7; AD 49) and his martyrdom in the mid-to-late 60s, but "ministry in Asia Minor, Greece, and Rome might very well have furnished Peter with a training in Greek, and even a rhetorical style, similar or even superior to that to be had in the classroom."[80] Finally, the use of a shorthand secretary (called an "amanuensis") was a common practice and may have influenced the style and final editing of a letter. In the case of 1 Peter, Silvanus (or Silas) seems to have been the amanuensis (1 Pet 5:12); there is no indication in 2 Peter whether an amanuensis was used.

- It is granted that 2 Peter was one of the last (if not the last) of the New Testament documents to be regarded as canonical, and it is not mentioned by name until Origen does so in the early third century. But there are many allusions to 2 Peter in earlier Christian writings, suggesting that the letter was fairly widely known and used from early on.[81]

- I hope that your encounter with 2 Peter has convinced you that it is completely unfair to stigmatize the letter as "harsh, even uncontrolled polemic offering only undisciplined rants against unorthodox Christian teachers."[82]

Of course, there is very much more that could be said about the authenticity of 2 Peter. In the final analysis, however, these are literary questions that do not ultimately detract from the value of 2 Peter as a canonical document. In giving these few pointers I hope to bolster your confidence that in reading and studying 2 Peter you are engaging a genuinely transformative word that will help you take your stand on the firm foundation God has given us in Christ, live in light of the coming end, and resist the seductions of false teaching that seeks to unsettle your faith.

RECOMMENDED READING

Despite the comparative neglect of the General Epistles, there is still a wide range of literature on 2 Peter, ranging from the very popular to the very arcane. Readers of the Transformative Word series who want to dig a little deeper into this intriguing letter might try the following as a next step:

Michael W. Goheen and Craig G. Bartholomew. *The True Story of the Whole World: Finding Your Place in the Biblical Drama,* revised edition. Grand Rapids: Brazos Press, 2020.

> A wonderfully accessible book about how the Bible, in six "acts" from creation and fall to the final restoration of all things, is God's true story of the whole world, and how followers of Christ can play their God-given role in this story.

Karen H. Jobes. *Letters to the Church: A Survey of Hebrews and the General Epistles.* Grand Rapids: Zondervan, 2011.

> As the title suggests, this book deals with all of the New Testament letters from Hebrews to Jude, including 2 Peter. It's a great place to start a more serious study of these letters. It provides an accessible, clearly written, and

beautifully illustrated treatment of these letters. I agree with the blurb by Mark Strauss on the back cover: "Jobes utilizes the best of biblical scholarship but presents it in a manner that beginning students will understand."

Douglas J. Moo. *2 Peter, Jude*. NIV Application Commentary. Grand Rapids: Zondervan, 1996.

This is a full-scale commentary by a seasoned New Testament scholar, but in keeping with the goals of the NIV Application Commentary series, it aims at determining the original meaning of a passage, bridging the gap between the world of the Bible and the world of today, and considering the contemporary significance of the text, with loads of practical application.

Ruth Anne Reese. *2 Peter and Jude*. Two Horizons New Testament Commentary. Grand Rapids: Eerdmans, 2007.

The Two Horizons New Testament Commentary series aims at combining "theological exegesis and theological reflection," and Reese's contribution to the series is a very fine example of what this entails, while remaining accessible, inspiring, and challenging.

NOTES

1. Quoted in Michael W. Goheen and Craig G. Bartholomew, *Living at the Crossroads: A Introduction to Christian Worldview* (Grand Rapids: Baker Academic, 2008), 5, emphasis added.

2. Bob Webber and Phil Kenyon, quoted in Craig G. Bartholomew and Michael W. Goheen, *The True Story of the Whole World: Finding Your Place in the Biblical Drama* (Grand Rapids: Faith Alive Christian Resources, 2009), 7, emphasis added.

3. Richard Foster has developed these themes at length in his book *Money, Sex and Power* (San Francisco: HarperCollins, 1987).

4. Increasingly, the value of understanding Scripture as the authentic "story" or metanarrative according to which Christ-followers should live their lives is being recognized. Among many helpful resources that focus on this way of understanding the Bible are Bartholomew and Goheen's *True Story of the Whole World*; J. Scott Duvall and J. Daniel Hays, *Living God's Word: Discovering Our Place in the Great Story of the Bible* (Grand Rapids: Zondervan, 2012), a companion volume to the same authors' *Grasping God's Word: A Hands-On Approach to Reading, Interpreting and Applying the Bible*, 3rd ed. (Grand Rapids: Zondervan, 2012); and Preben Vang and Terry G. Carter, *Telling God's Story: The Biblical Narrative from Beginning to End*, 2nd ed. (Nashville: B&H Academic, 2013). For those who want to dig (considerably!) deeper, Kevin J. Vanhoozer's book *The Drama of Doctrine: A Canonical-Linguistic Approach to Christian Doctrine* (Louisville: Westminster John Knox, 2005) is an excellent resource, approaching the biblical story (as the title implies) as a drama.

5. This quote is ascribed to D. L. Moody on many websites, although I have not been able to document the precise source.

6. So, for example, Ruth Anne Reese, *2 Peter and Jude*, Two Horizons New Testament Commentary (Grand Rapids: Eerdmans, 2007), 201–2.

7. I'm grateful to Amy Richter for her sermon "The Gift of Words," *Expository Times* 126, no. 11 (Aug 2015): 545, where this illustration appears.

8. Peter Davids, *A Theology of James, Peter, and Jude* (Grand Rapids: Zondervan, 2014), 190.

9. Helpful examples from recent literature on the General Letters include Karen Jobes, *Letters to the Church: A Survey of Hebrews and the General Epistles* (Grand Rapids: Zondervan, 2011); Davids, *Theology of James, Peter, and Jude*; and a spate of new commentaries on individual letters. Advocating convincingly the idea that the General Letters are best understood as a "canonical collection" are David R. Nienhuis and Robert W. Wall, *Reading the Epistles of James, Peter, John, and Jude as Scripture: The Shaping and Shape of a Canonical Collection* (Grand Rapids: Eerdmans, 2013); and Darian Lockett, *An Introduction to the Catholic Epistles* (New York: T&T Clark, 2012).

10. If you are interested in exploring these issues in more detail, see the appendix for an introductory discussion of some of the critical issues connected to the study of 2 Peter.

11. Lockett, *Introduction to the Catholic Epistles*, 76.

12. Joel B. Green, "Cultivating the Practice of Reading Scripture," Catalyst Resources, February 5, 2014, www.catalystresources.org/cultivating-the-practice -of-reading-scripture.

13. As I pointed out in the introduction, most scholars, including many evangelicals, have raised significant questions about whether the apostle Peter himself was—or could have been—the author of this letter. In my opinion, there is nothing that definitively rules Peter out of the equation as the author, and the questions raised against Peter's authorship are not insurmountable, even though they are difficult. Either way, I will refer to the author as "Peter" throughout this book. N. T. Wright offers a helpful comment on this score: "Some people doubt that what we call 2 Peter was written by Peter himself, but several parts of it indicate that it is indeed supposed to come from him in

some sense, even if he didn't physically write it himself." See Wright, *1 & 2 Peter and Jude: Nine Studies for Individuals and Groups* (Downers Grove, IL: InterVarsity, 2012). For further discussion of this question and its implications, see the appendix.

14. Clement, bishop of the church at Rome near the end of the first century, wrote in about AD 96, "Peter, who because of unrighteous jealousy endured not one or two but many trials, and thus having given his testimony went to his appointed place in glory." See 1 Clement 5.4 in Michael W. Holmes, *The Apostolic Fathers: Greek Texts with English Translations*, 3rd ed. (Grand Rapids: Baker Academic, 2007), 51. The Greek word translated "given his testimony" is *martyreō*, whence we derive our English word "martyr." In his *Church History* 3.1 (ca. AD 324), the early church historian Eusebius reflects the tradition that "Peter seems to have preached to the Jews of the Dispersion in Pontus, Galatia, Bithynia, Cappadocia, and Asia. Finally, he came to Rome and was crucified, head downward at his own request." See Paul L. Maier, trans., *Eusebius: The Church History* (Grand Rapids: Kregel, 2007), 80. For more information on Peter, consult a good Bible dictionary, such as *Lexham Bible Dictionary*.

15. *Amistad*, directed by Steven Spielberg (DreamWorks, 1997); *Twelve Years a Slave*, directed by Steve McQueen (River Road, Plan B, and New Regency, 2013).

16. Does the expression "our God and Savior Jesus Christ" (2 Pet 1:1) refer to two persons (God, and our Savior Jesus Christ) or just one (Jesus Christ, who is our God and Savior)? You can see how important the question is, because if the second option is correct, Peter is affirming the full deity of Jesus Christ. Greek grammarian Granville Sharp (1735–1813), who was also a campaigner against the slave trade, formulated a grammatical rule that has come to bear his name: the Granville Sharp rule. According to this rule, where two nouns describing a person (but not personal names such as Peter or Paul) are joined by "and," and only the first noun has the definite article "the," both nouns refer to the same person. In 2 Pet 1:1, the word order in the original Greek reads like this: "the God of-us and Savior Jesus Christ." You can see how this construction fits Granville Sharp's criteria: the

first noun, "God," has the article "the," whereas the second, "Savior," does not, and the two nouns are joined by "and." So both nouns, "God" and "Savior," are referring to the same person, Jesus Christ, thus affirming that Jesus Christ is both God and Savior. Other examples in 2 Peter include 1:11 and 2:20, both of which read "our Lord and Savior Jesus Christ." Another classic instance of the Granville Sharp rule is in Titus 2:13, "our great God and Savior, Jesus Christ."

17. "For a Christian writer around 100 CE to say, 'you may become participants of the divine nature' (2 Pet 1:4), was to evoke not only biblical images, but also concepts of divinization that were central to the leading Hellenistic philosophies—Middle-Platonism and Stoicism. Of course, Second Peter's is a Christian teaching, but here he uses terminology that is recognizable from the Greek philosophical traditions, and this should not be overlooked in studies of 2 Peter." Steven Finlan, "Second Peter's Notion of Divine Participation," in *Theōsis: Deification in Christian Theology*, ed. Stephen Finlan and Vladimir Karmalov (Eugene, OR: Pickwick, 2006), 1:32.

18. See Become a Living God, http://www.becomealivinggod.com/spellcasting/secret-psychology-becoming-living-god.php. Or take as another example this rendering of an ancient Buddhist story:

> A doll of salt, after a long pilgrimage on dry land, came to the sea and discovered something she had never seen and could not possibly understand. She stood on the firm ground, a solid little doll of salt, and saw there was another ground that was mobile, insecure, noisy, strange and unknown. She asked the sea, *"But what are you?"* and it said, *"I am the sea."* And the doll said, *"What is the sea?"* to which the answer was, *"It is me."* Then the doll said, *"I cannot understand, but I want to; how can I?"* The sea answered, *"Touch me."* So the doll shyly put forward a foot and touched the water and she got a strange impression that it was something that began to be knowable. She withdrew her leg, looked and saw that her toes had gone, and she was afraid and said, *"Oh, but where is my toe, what have you done to me?"* And the sea said, *"You have given something in order to understand."* Gradually the water took away small bits of the

doll's salt and the doll went farther and farther into the sea and at every moment she had a sense of understanding more and more, and yet of not being able to say what the sea was. As she went deeper, she melted more and more, repeating: *"But what is the sea?"* At last a wave dissolved the rest of her and the doll said: *"It is I!"* (As recounted by Anthony Bloom in *Living Prayer* [London: Darton, Longman and Todd, 1966], 105–6)

19. Eastern Orthodox churches have always paid more attention to deification than have the churches of the West, but interest in the idea has been growing over the last decade or so. Convenient means of entering the discussion are Finlan and Karmalov, *Theōsis*, vol. 1 ; Vladimir Karmalov, ed., *Theōsis: Deification in Christian Theology*, vol. 2 (Eugene, OR: Pickwick, 2011). Particularly helpful in the first volume are Finlan and Kharmalov, "Introduction," 1–15; Finlan, "Second Peter's Notion of Divine Participation," 32–50; Myk Habets, "Reforming Theôsis," 146–67. J. Todd Billings has written a thoughtful article, "United to God through Christ: Assessing Calvin on the Question of Deification," *Harvard Theological Review* 98 (2005): 315–34.

20. Michael J. Gorman, *Becoming the Gospel: Paul, Participation, and Mission* (Grand Rapids: Eerdmans, 2015), 4.

21. Views reported by Peter Davids in *The Letters of 2 Peter and Jude* (Grand Rapids: Eerdmans, 2006), 121–22, though not his own viewpoint.

22. Quoted in John Dillenberger, *Luther: Selections from His Works* (New York: Anchor, 1962), 492.

23. Desiring God, "Horton: 'Grace is not opposed to human activity. It's opposed to human merit.' #DGPasCon," February 4, 2014, https://twitter.com/desiringgod/status/430752286776651776.

24. Didache 1.1, in Holmes, *Apostolic Fathers*, 345.

25. D. A. Carson, *For the Love of God: A Daily Companion for Discovering the Riches of God's Word* (Wheaton: Crossway, 2006), 2:23.

26. Moisés Silva, *New International Dictionary of New Testament Theology and Exegesis*, 2nd ed. (Grand Rapids: Zondervan, 2014), 2:85. The technical term for such lists, also found in the classical world, is *sorites*.

27. Richard J. Bauckham, *Jude, 2 Peter*, Word Biblical Commentary (Waco: Word, 1983), 187.

28. A. T. Robertson suggests that the word "add" used here means "to fit out the chorus with additional (complete) supplies." See Robertson, *Word Pictures in the New Testament*, vol. 6, The General Epistles and the Revelation of John (Nashville: Broadman, 1933). It was only a short step from there to the imagery of a choir adding harmony to a melody. I'm grateful to my colleague Neil Bernard for suggesting this connection.

29. Frederick William Danker, *The Concise Greek-English Lexicon of the New Testament* (Chicago: University of Chicago Press, 2009), 53.

30. Peter H. Davids, *2 Peter and Jude: A Handbook on the Greek Text* (Waco: Baylor University Press, 2011), 47.

31. Bauckham, *Jude, 2 Peter*, 186.

32. Quoted in Gene L. Green, *Jude and 2 Peter*, Baker Exegetical Commentary on the New Testament (Grand Rapids: Baker Academic, 2008), 193.

33. Green, *Jude and 2 Peter*, 194.

34. Davids, *Letters of 2 Peter and Jude*, 184.

35. Don Francisco, "Love Is Not a Feeling," *Holiness* (Newpax, 1984).

36. For example, the list of challenging Christian biographies includes classics such as Augustine's *Confessions*, Corrie ten Boom's *The Hiding Place*, Elisabeth Elliot's *Through Gates of Splendor*, and Paul Hattaway's *The Heavenly Man: The Remarkable True Story of Chinese Christian Brother Yun*. See Goodreads, "Best Christian Biography/Autobiography," http://www.goodreads.com/list/show/16480.Best _Christian_Biography_Autobiography. This is only a small sampling of a great feast.

37. Thomas à Kempis, *The Imitation of Christ* (Alachua, FL: Bridge-Logos, 1999), 23.

38. *The Lord of the Rings: The Fellowship of the Ring*, directed by Peter Jackson (New Line Cinema and Wingnut Films, 2011).

39. In reflecting on his imminent death and wanting his readers to remember his teaching after he has gone, Peter

adopts a familiar style known in the ancient Jewish world as a "testament." For further discussion of the testament as a literary genre and its implications for our interpretation of 2 Peter, see the appendix.

40. Robertson, *Word Pictures*, 6:154.

41. James D. G. Dunn, *Christianity in the Making*, vol. 1, *Jesus Remembered* (Grand Rapids: Eerdmans, 2003), 179.

42. There are many useful tools for memorizing Scripture. See, for example, Andrew M. Davis, *An Approach to Extended Memorization of Scripture* (Greenville, SC: Ambassador International, 2014), also available as an ebook. For many years, The Navigators have encouraged Scripture memorization through their Topical Memory System; see https://www.navigators.org/resource/topical-memory-system.

43. Davids, *Letters of 2 Peter and Jude*, 191; Davids, *2 Peter and Jude*, 52.

44. Davids, *Letters of 2 Peter and Jude*, 193.

45. Irenaeus, *Against Heresies* 3.4, my paraphrase.

46. In Jewish use, the term "prophetic word" was applicable to any part of the Old Testament. See Max Zerwick and Mary Grosvenor, *A Grammatical Analysis of the Greek New Testament* (Rome: Biblical Institute Press, 1981), 719.

47. In the early 1200s Archbishop Stephen Langton devised the chapter divisions we use today, and the verse numbering system familiar to us first appeared in Robert Estienne's 1551 edition of the Greek New Testament.

48. *Dekalog* (1989), Telewizja Polska; Australian edition released on DVD in 2005 by Umbrella World Cinema.

49. Annette Insdorf, *Double Lives, Second Chances: The Cinema of Krzysztof Kieslowski* (New York: Hyperion, 1999), 74.

50. A persistent question in General Epistles scholarship is the relationship of 2 Peter to Jude, since much of the material in 2 Pet 2–3 parallels the content of Jude. See the appendix for further information.

51. Proposals have included gnostics, Epicureans, and an "unknown group." See, for example, Davids, *Theology of James, Peter and Jude*, 192–99. The most that can be said with confidence is that certain aspects of gnostic and Epicurean

teaching parallel that of the false teachers in 2 Peter. But there is little unanimity on the issue of who precisely the opponents in 2 Peter actually are.

52. "Objections": Bauckham, *Jude, 2 Peter*, 135; "accusations": Duane F. Watson, *Invention, Arrangement, and Style: Rhetorical Criticism of Jude and 2 Peter*, Society of Biblical Literature Dissertation Series 104 (Atlanta: Scholars, 1988), 141–42.

53. Jobes, *Letters to the Church*, 370. Watson provides the following fuller description of the objections and accusations of the false teachers in 2 Peter: "The apostolic proclamation of the parousia [second coming of Christ] is a cleverly devised myth" (2 Pet 1:16a); "the Old Testament prophecy upon which the apostles base their teaching of the parousia are matters of the prophet's own interpretations and impulse, not that of the Holy Spirit" (2 Pet 1:20b–21a); "divine judgment is 'idle' and 'asleep' " (2 Pet 2:3b; see 3:9); "the apostolic preaching of an imminent parousia is to be denied on the basis of the death of the first generation of Christians who were prophesied would experience it, and on the basis of the lack of divine intervention in history" (2 Pet 3:3–4) (Invention, Arrangement, and Style, 141–42).

54. Peter's description here suggests that the false teachers may originally have belonged to the Christian faith but apostasized from it. See further the discussion on 2 Pet 2:19–22.

55. A number of difficult questions arise in connection with 2 Pet 2:4–10a. They include the following:

Who precisely are the angels who sinned (2 Pet 2:4)? While some interpreters have made a connection between this verse and the fall of Satan and his angels perhaps described in Isa 14:12–17 and Ezek 28:11–19, it seems more likely that the reference is to the contemporary Jewish interpretation of the "sons of God" (angels) who mated with "the daughters of men" (Gen 6:1–3), an explanation that fits in with the pseudepigraphical Jewish work 1 Enoch, dating from about the third century BC. If so, Peter would be referring to a widely accepted understanding that the activity of these sinful angels led inevitably to judgment. Jude similarly refers to 1 Enoch (Jude 14–15).

What does it mean that God sent these sinful angels to "hell" (2 Pet 2:4)? "Hell" is the translation given in most English versions of this verse, but this translation is questionable. The Greek text reads that God confined them to Tartarus—literally, that he "Tartarus-ed" them. A familiar term in both Greek pagan religion and Second Temple Judaism (but used only here in the New Testament), Tartarus referred to a subterranean place where evil spirits were confined until the coming day of judgment. So, unlike most conceptions of hell, Tartarus is not the final destination of the unrighteous but a temporary holding cell until the final judgement, a concept confirmed in 2 Pet 2:9b, "the Lord knows how ... to hold the unrighteous for punishment on the day of judgment." Once again, the point that Peter emphasizes, contrary to the opinion of the false teachers, is that judgment of evil is inevitable.

Why is Lot referred to as "righteous" (2 Pet 2:7)? Lot doesn't exactly cover himself with glory in the Genesis account (Gen 13; 19), being depicted as a somewhat selfish and spineless character. In his favor, however, Lot is "distressed" and "tormented" by the unrestrained evil of the cities of Sodom and Gomorrah (2 Pet 2:7-8), and some contemporary Jewish writings (such as Wisdom of Solomon 10:6; 19:17) also refer to him as "righteous." Thus, in Peter's argument, Lot's escape from Sodom (Gen 19:12-29) serves as a paradigm for God's deliverance of the righteous, in contrast to the impending judgment of the unrighteous.

The answers to questions such as these may not always be definitive, but the big picture is clear: God will surely bring judgment on the unrighteous, but just as surely he will deliver the righteous.

56. The traditional and most obvious view is that if 2 Peter is the "second letter," then 1 Peter must be the first and the apostle Peter is the author of both of the New Testament letters that bear his name. For a variety of reasons, many contemporary scholars (including some evangelicals) doubt that the apostle Peter was the author of 2 Peter, thus making uncertain the identity of the first letter referred to here (some suggest Jude, others another unknown letter written earlier to the same recipients as 2 Peter). In my opinion, the reasons usually advanced for rejecting Petrine authorship are not watertight. Thus I take at face value the identification of the apostle Peter as the author of both let-

ters (1 Pet 1:1; 2 Pet 1:1), while acknowledging at the same time that there are plenty of unanswered questions. For further discussion on this and other critical matters, see the appendix.

57. Mark A. Noll, *The Scandal of the Evangelical Mind* (Grand Rapids: Eerdmans, 1994), 3.

58. Quoted in James W. Sire, *Discipleship of the Mind: Learning to Love God in the Ways We Think* (Downers Grove, IL: InterVarsity Press, 1990), 12. Dealing with a similar theme is Sire, *Habits of the Mind: Intellectual Life as a Christian Calling* (Downers Grove, IL: InterVarsity Press, 2000).

59. Davids, *2 Peter and Jude*, 92.

60. An enormous theological debate swirls around 2 Pet 3:9. If it is God's desire that no one should perish, why is it that many do in fact perish? The answer to this question generally settles into one of two alternative types. Some emphasize the free will of human beings: it is not God's desire that any should perish, but because rebellious people choose of their own free will to turn their backs on God, they end up perishing. Others argue that God has chosen only a specific group for salvation ("the elect"), and in light of a verse such as 2 Pet 3:9 they make a distinction between God's "desiderative" will (what he desires—the salvation of all) and his "effective" will (what actually does happen—the salvation of the elect only). Still others argue that "everybody" in this verse "must refer to members of the audience who have repented or will soon repent." See Steven J. Kraftchick, Jude, 2 Peter (Nashville: Abingdon, 2002), 162. None of these views is without difficulty, and this is not the place to attempt to settle the debate. It is clear enough, however, that God takes no pleasure in the death of the wicked (see, for example, Ezek 18:23, 32; 33:11) and that the delay in the judgment is due to God's patience in allowing more time to repent. For a brief and accessible discussion on the debate, see (for example) Douglas J. Moo, 2 Peter, Jude, NIV Application Commentary (Grand Rapids: Zondervan, 1996), 187–88.

61. Stephen R. Covey, *The Seven Habits of Highly Effective People* (New York: Simon & Schuster, 1989), 98.

62. Green, *Jude and 2 Peter*, 332, emphasis added. Among the New Testament passages mentioned by Green in this connection are Mark 13:32–37; Rom 13:12; Phil 4:5; 1 Thess 5:1–11; 2 Tim 4:1–2; Jas 5:8–9; 1 Pet 1:13–17, 4:7; 1 John 2:28.

63. Reese, *2 Peter and Jude*, 201–2.

64. Kraftchick, *Jude, 2 Peter*, 168.

65. Matthew Y. Emerson, "Does God Own a Death Star? The Destruction of the Cosmos in 2 Peter 3:1–13," *Southwestern Journal of Theology* 57 (Spring 2015): 281–93. Emerson shows that "Peter does not use the phrase 'pass away' to denote annihilation; Peter uses the fire imagery to speak of refinement, not annihilation; Peter uses the flood comparison [2 Pet 5–6] to speak of purification, not annihilation; and Peter writes within a canonical framework that includes a theology of God's good creation and his promised redemption of it" (285). See also N. T. Wright, *Surprised by Hope* (London: SPCK, 2007); J. Richard Middleton, *A New Heaven and a New Earth: Reclaiming Biblical Eschatology* (Grand Rapids: Baker Academic, 2014).

66. N. T. Wright, *The Early Christian Letters for Everyone: James, Peter, John, and Judah* (Louisville: Westminster John Knox, 2011), 119. See also the important article by Albert Wolters, "Worldview and Textual Criticism in 2 Peter 3:10," *Westminster Theological Journal* 49 (1987): 405–13.

67. Wright, *Early Christian Letters*, 119.

68. Galatians 2:11–14 records a sharp disagreement between Paul and Peter ("Cephas"; see John 1:42). It is popular in some quarters of New Testament scholarship to see this disagreement as representative of a permanent and bitter division between Peter and Paul, and, further, that since the conflict was so sharp, someone other than the real Peter must be the author of 2 Peter, because the real Peter would never have been able to refer to Paul as "our dear brother Paul" (2 Pet 3:15). But such a conclusion is unwarranted. Not only does it overlook the reconciling power of the gospel, but it ignores the fact that as apostles Peter and Paul were preaching the same essential message (the parallels between the letters of Peter on the one hand and those of Paul on the other are far more dominant than their

occasional differences in emphasis). Peter's practice did not always keep up with his theology, and he needed the occasional prod from people such as Paul. But it is unwarranted to posit a permanent breach between them on these grounds.

69. Peter uses two different Greek words for "knowledge" in this letter: *gnōsis* and *epignōsis*. The former tends toward a factual knowledge (here and in 2 Pet 1:5–6), whereas the latter has the connotation of personal, experiential knowledge (2 Pet 1:2–3, 8; 2:20). Probably the distinction between these two words should not be pressed too far, and Christians are called to grow both in their knowledge base about Jesus Christ and in their personal experience of him.

70. Project Gutenberg E-text of *The Pilgrim's Progress*, by John Bunyan, https://www.gutenberg.org/files/131/131-h/131-h.htm.

71. Donald Guthrie, *New Testament Introduction* (London: Inter-Varsity Press, 1970), 814.

72. Particularly by Bauckham in his important contribution to the Word Biblical Commentary series, *Jude, 2 Peter*, especially 131–35.

73. Lockett's description in *Introduction to the Catholic Epistles*, 76, although this is not a viewpoint he shares.

74. In Ernst Käsemann's programmatic essay, "An Apologia for Primitive Christian Eschatology," in *Essays on New Testament Themes*, trans. W. J. Montague, Studies in Biblical Theology 41 (London: SCM, 1964), 169.

75. Davids, *Letters of 2 Peter and Jude*, 121; Davids, *Theology of James, Peter, and Jude*, 189.

76. I mention these two articles because they are easily accessible online. See Michael J. Kruger, "The Authenticity of 2 Peter," Biblical Studies, https://www.etsjets.org/files/JETS-PDFs/42/42-4/42-4-pp645-671_JETS.pdf. The article first appeared in *Journal of the Evangelical Theological Society* 42.4 (1999). See also Daniel B. Wallace, "Second Peter: Introduction, Argument, and Outline," Bible.org, https://bible.org/seriespage/22-second-peter-introduction-argument-and-outline.

77. Many English versions simply render the name as "Simon" in both 2 Pet 1:1 and Acts 15:14, presumably to avoid confusion. The NIV has an explanatory footnote at Acts 15:14, "Greek Simeon, a variant of Simon; that is, Peter," but puzzlingly neglects to do the same at 2 Pet 1:1.

78. D. A. Carson and Douglas J. Moo, *An Introduction to the New Testament*, 2nd ed. (Grand Rapids: Zondervan, 2005), 662–63.

79. It may be significant that the Greeks who came to worship in Jerusalem approached one of the disciples, Philip, "from Bethsaida in Galilee" (John 12:20–21), with the request to see Jesus—perhaps because as a Galilean he would have been able to understand Greek? See my article, "Was Peter Capable of Writing the Greek of 2 Peter? An Exploration," Crucible Online, http://www.crucibleonline.net/wp-content/uploads/2016/08/Morcom-Authorship-of-2-Peter-2.pdf.

80. Carson and Moo, *Introduction to the New Testament*, 661.

81. See further Kruger, "Authenticity of 2 Peter"; Wallace, "Second Peter."

82. Lockett, *Introduction to the Catholic Epistles*, 76.

LEXHAM PRESS

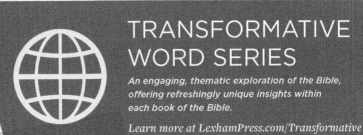

TRANSFORMATIVE WORD SERIES

An engaging, thematic exploration of the Bible, offering refreshingly unique insights within each book of the Bible.

Learn more at LexhamPress.com/Transformative

Revealing the Heart of
Prayer
The Gospel of Luke

CRAIG BARTHOLOMEW

2 CORINTHIANS

CUTTING TIES WITH DARKNESS

JOHN D. BARRY

TO

SS
ONE
EVELATION

Y. EMERSON

THE BOOK OF ESTHER

God Behind the Scenes
WAYNE BARKHUIZEN

When You Want to YELL AT GOD

The Book of Job
Craig Bartholomew